5 Marks of Devotion to God

by C. Matthew McMahon

Copyright Information

Table of Contents

Introduction

"Let us draw near with a true heart in full assurance of faith," (Heb. 10:22).

Do you long to be closer in your relationship to Jesus Christ? Do you desire a more intimate communion with God? *Every* true Christian does. When considering how one comes closer to Christ, there are a number of constituted means by which God uses to draw *his people* into a more intimate awareness of both his person and work. These are deemed, "the means of grace." The means of grace are those opportunities which God has instituted to draw closer to him. They are a means by which God is more fully experienced through the work of Jesus Christ, in the power of the Spirit. Such means are those activities that God is "in" and will minister grace to his people as he so deems fit.[1] God has prescribed certain duties to Christians that they may perform by the power of Christ's Spirit so that God may use those means as a conduit for grace ministered to them.

Some activities that churches employ might be helpful in some other way but are not part of the prescribed means of grace. If a church has a Jazzercise group that meets on Wednesday mornings to exercise, that might be helpful to one's physical well-being, but

---

[1] "God is a Spirit: and they that worship him must worship him in spirit and in truth," (John 4:24).

that is not a constituted means by which God prescribed grace through Christ in worship.[2] *The means of grace* are found in the preaching of the word, the sacraments, prayer, reading and studying the Bible, godly meditation, Christian fellowship, and biblical worship. They are the constituted means by which Christians draw closer in their relationship with Christ. Jonathan Edwards said, "The word and ordinances and works of God are means of grace, as they give opportunity for the proper and fit exercise of grace, and are in a sort means of that exercise."[3]

When looking at the means of grace, they can be divided into two primary sections: worship in church and worship at home; or as the *1647 Westminster Confession of Faith* separates them, public worship and private worship. The purpose of this volume in the *5*

---

[2] "By means of grace are not meant every instrumentality which God may please to make the means of spiritual edification to his children. The phrase is intended to indicate those institutions which God has ordained to be the ordinary channels of grace, *i.e.*, of the supernatural influences of the Holy Spirit, to the souls of men." Hodge, Charles, *Systematic Theology*, Volume 3, (Oak Harbor, WA: Logos Research Systems, Inc., 1997) 466. Also, "The means of grace are means of sanctification. They suppose the existence of the principle of divine life in the soul: "The outward and ordinary means whereby Christ communicates to his church the benefits of his mediation are all his ordinances; especially the word, sacraments, and prayer; all of which are made effectual to the elect for their salvation" (Westminster Larger Catechism 154)." Shedd, W. G. T., *Dogmatic Theology*. A.W. Gomes, Ed., 3rd, (Phillipsburg, NJ: P & R Pub. 2003), 809.
[3] Edwards, Jonathan, *The Works of Jonathan Edwards*, The "Miscellanies": (Entry Nos. 501–832). A. Chamberlain & H. S. Stout, Eds., Volume 18, (New Haven; London: Yale University Press, 2000) 157.

Marks series is to cover the spiritual disciplines housed in private devotions. It not enough to merely know about "devotions" in some ethereal manner, but how bible doctrine works its way practically into the life of the believer to further conform them into the image of their only Savior Jesus Christ. It is to come to know God in a deeper manner, and to be empowered by the Spirit of God for the glory of Christ (Romans 8:29 and 12:2), and to mortify the remaining sin that impedes our walk with God. As Anthony Burgess rightly concluded, "the more we have the means of grace to set us at liberty, the more doth our slavery discover itself."[4]

This work is going to lead you, reader, to consider the biblical methods of drawing closer to God, and cultivating the spiritual disciplines of bible reading and study, prayer, godly meditation, fasting and family worship. There you have the *5 marks* of biblical devotion to God as it pertains to private worship in the home. These are those means which God has prescribed and ordained for the end of communicating the life-giving and sanctifying influences of the Spirit to the souls of men.[5] As Luther rightly remarked, "By means of these God shows us, as by a visible sign, that he is with us, takes care of us, and is favorably inclined toward us."[6] In this way, the means of grace are precious and should not

---

[4] Burgess, Anthony, *A Treatise of Original Sin*, (London: s.n., 1658), 319.
[5] See Hodge on prayer in his *Systematic Theology*, 708.
[6] Luther, Martin, *Luther's Works*, Volume 1, (Saint Louis: Concordia Publishing House., 1999) 309.

be taken for granted as many do, because God condescends (i.e. stoops down to save), only at special times to renew the outpourings of his Spirit, and revive his people. With this in mind, consider your own devotions and private worship in your families.

How would you describe your personal devotions now? Be specific in your thoughts about it. How do you incorporate prayer, bible reading, bible study and godly meditation now as part of your personal daily devotions? Do you fast? Are your prayers cold or lively? Do you study the bible or just read it? Do you meditate on the word at all? Do you know what godly meditation is? Consider your personal devotions over the last week. How do they differ from how they are going this week? How are they the same? How long do you spend in devotions each day? How have you grown this week in your Christian faith in comparison to last week? Are you trying to grow? Is your devotional life better this month than last month? Or last year?

The goal in all this is not to be good stewards of merely *going through the motions*. The goal in this study is to love God and Jesus Christ more today than you did yesterday. These exercises work themselves out daily. But they are only as helpful as you are thoughtful and dedicated. It's not about simply flexing your theological muscles each day. It is primarily to gain the real blessing of the Spirit, further conformity to the image of Jesus Christ, and a deeper fellowship with the Father. What real Christian doesn't want *that?*

The first conviction that you must have in dealing effectively and biblically with your personal devotions (assuming that you are a truly converted Christian) is committing to having personal devotions daily. There is a twofold consideration on this point which is exceedingly important. The first is that God commands his people concerning a daily time of devotions. The second consideration is that Christians ought to see personal devotions as a delight, not as a burden. If Joshua 1:8-9, Psalm 1:2 and 1 Thessalonians 5:17 were the only 3 Scriptures in all the bible that direct Christians to pray, read and meditate through God's word, *they would be enough.* But there are literally myriads of bible passages in which God commands, over and over, the duty of bible reading, prayer, pondering the word of God, fasting and family worship.

It is relatively impossible to sit comfortably on a stool with only two legs. Most Christians (1) read a passage of Scripture, or a verse in some "daily devotional", and then (2) offer up a few prayers of things they need or want to God, and believe they have fulfilled their "personal devotion" time, much less taken time to spend in family worship each day. Or, for that matter, they have yet to put down the pizza in order to pick up fasting once a week. They may have never been taught that the stool of spiritual discipline in relationship to personal devotions comprises, first, of three legs. Bible reading, godly meditation and prayer are all necessary prerequisites for a successful daily time of personal devotions. And then one must consider how they interact with family worship each day. And then after that, there should be a time where the Christian is employed in denying "self" and fasting for their good and spiritual well-being. These spiritual disciplines are necessary to fulfill what God has specifically commanded, as we will see.

It could be your personal devotions are unstructured, undisciplined, and unworthy of being called spiritual *disciplines*. "It is a very amiable thing when persons that profess religion, are lively and active in religion."[7] Cultivating a personal relationship with God takes *work*. So, in considering the basics of these 5 marks, let's start with devotions surrounding the word of God.

---

[7] Edwards, Jonathan, The Amiableness of Liveliness in Religion. In W. H. Kimnach, Ed., *Jonathan Edwards Sermons,* (New Haven, CT: The Jonathan Edwards Center at Yale University, 2016) electronic ed.

Mark 1: Daily Bible Reading

"These were more noble than those in Thessalonica, in that they received the word with all readiness of mind, and searched the scriptures *daily*, whether those things were so," (Acts 17:11).

The context of Acts 17:11 falls within the scope of Paul's second missionary journey. Paul began at Jerusalem with Silas, to travel back to Galatia and visit churches which had been planted. "Now when they had passed through Amphipolis and Apollonia, they came to Thessalonica, where there was a synagogue of the Jews," (Acts 17:1). At this point, Timothy would have joined them at Lystra, and together they went through Macedonia and Achaia, which is modern day Greece.

"Then Paul, as his custom was, went in to them, and for three Sabbaths reasoned with them from the Scriptures, explaining and demonstrating that the Christ had to suffer and rise again from the dead, and saying, "This Jesus whom I preach to you is the Christ.""" (Acts 17:2-3). Paul was there for at least three weeks, and it seems (from verses 6-9) a brother, by the name of Jason, put them up for this time in order that Paul could reason with the Jews in the synagogues.

As a note, synagogues operated in their worship in the following manner, which should be helpful to all those that would like to know what the template was for church-worship under the Christian banner. There was an initial blessing or invocation surrounding worship and the attributes of God. Next the "psalms" section occurred where they were sung, and also used for prayer. Next was the *Amidah* (meaning *standing*) where there would be given the 18 blessings, and then a silent prayer was personally encouraged. Then came the reading of the Torah, and a prayer. Then came the sermon. Then finally the blessing. Then the *Kiddush* occurred, which was a blessing over the wine in the sabbath hall for fellowship. It is *here* that Paul would have reasoned with them.

"And some of them were persuaded; and a great multitude of the devout Greeks, and not a few of the leading women, joined Paul and Silas," (Acts 17:4). It's noted here by the writer, which is Luke, some were persuaded, some being devout Greeks, and leading women. There seems to be here in this chapter an emphasis of sorts, on *respectable* or *notable* people. They were leading women, and devout Greeks.

"But the Jews who were not persuaded, becoming envious, took some of the evil men from the marketplace, and gathering a mob, set all the city in an uproar and attacked the house of Jason, and sought to bring them out to the people," (Acts 17:5). There are two kinds of people here, believers *and* unbelievers that emerge from this work of the apostle in the synagogue. The believers believed, and the unbelievers gathered a mob to attack the apostle and his group.

"But when they did not find them, they dragged Jason and some brethren to the rulers of the city, crying out, "These who have turned the world upside down have come here too. "Jason has harbored them, and these are all acting contrary to the decrees of Caesar, saying there is another king – Jesus." And they troubled the crowd and the rulers of the city when they heard these things. So when they had taken security from Jason and the rest, they let them go," (Acts 17:6-9). Interestingly, these unbelievers testify that the apostles, through Christ, in the uproar that has taken place since the resurrection, have *turned the world upside down*. They disparage this action and work. They desire *their kingdom* more than God's, and wanted to put an end to them and this upbraiding of their kingdom of choice.

"Then the brethren immediately sent Paul and Silas away by night to Berea. When they arrived, they went into the synagogue of the Jews," (Acts 17:10). They sent Paul and Silas away, fearing they would be killed by the mob, and they are found to move on into Berea. This was about fifty miles away from where they were. Again, Paul, as was his custom, went into the synagogue there to reason with them.

"These were more fair-minded than those in Thessalonica, in that they received the word with all readiness, and searched the Scriptures daily to find out whether these things were so. Therefore many of them believed, and also not a few of the Greeks, prominent women as well as men," (Acts 17:11-12). We find Luke, again, mentioning *prominent* people, and those of nobility in the synagogue. These people seemed primed and ready to study whatever the rabbis taught in the synagogue to be sure it lined up with Scripture. They were not only noble because they study, but, they are noble *to study.* This noble birth enabled these prominent people in Berea to study the Scriptures daily. Whatever their classical education might have been, of noble birth, they had the ability to know how to study. How long were Paul and Silas there? There is no note on their stay this time. It was long enough for Luke to use a very important word for biblical study, which is the word "daily,"[1] and also long enough for the conversion of not a few people. Then comes trouble.

"But when the Jews from Thessalonica learned that the word of God was preached by Paul at Berea, they came there also and stirred up the crowds. Then immediately the brethren sent Paul away, to go to the sea; but both Silas and Timothy remained there. So those who conducted Paul brought him to Athens; and receiving a command for Silas and Timothy to come to him with all speed, they departed," (Acts 17:13-15). When the murderous unbelievers found that the stir was occurring just fifty miles south, (not far enough from them) they took it upon themselves to go there as well and stop this preaching that turns the world upside down. For a time, Timothy and Silas stayed, but Paul departed. It seems that these noble students of the word

---

[1] τὸ καθ᾽ ἡμέραν ἀνακρίνοντες τὰς γραφάς (Acts 17:11). *Daily.*

needed a bit more help and bit more pastoral ministry, so to speak, until Paul called for Silas and Timothy to come to Athens.

More specifically, consider Acts 17:11, where it begins with "these..." Who were "these?" They were the Bereans. Who "... were more fair-minded than those in Thessalonica." *Fair-minded* is somewhat of a poor translation. They were "more noble."[2] Why would Luke think this is important? Why would the Holy Spirit single out one group over another in this way? What qualities could one discern from observing those of prominence and nobility? In this particular context it is extremely important. They were in fact, educated to a certain degree, and they studied *every day*. But nobility is used here not only of the possibility of being of noble or high in their birth, which would fit with Luke's use of the prominent people he mentions in both Thessalonica and Berea, but it used in the clause as an adjective which is descriptive based on the latter part of the verse. "... in that they received the word with all readiness." They had the word. They *took the word by the hand*, or literally, *received* it. They did this with all *readiness*, or more literally, *zealously with an open mind*. They were noble not only in class, but as those singled out by the Holy Spirit who took the word of God by the hand, as it were, with zeal and eagerness, and what did they do? "... and searched...." They examined it. This searching or

---

[2] εὐγενέστεροι means noble, or, from the root word meaning *born well* as it is in relationship to a family; *i.e.* of the best of families.

examination is akin to Laban searching the tents for his stolen household gods in Gen. 31:34. Searching the heart of David by God in Psalm 139:1. Searching the heart of the preacher in Ecclesiastes 2:3, as to how he would gratify his flesh in his worldly experiment. And in 1 Peter 1:10, it is used of the prophets who searched carefully of the prophesied grace to come in Jesus Christ. They were searching the Scriptures diligently, eagerly, grasping it by the hand.

What, exactly, did they search? "...the Scriptures." The *graphe* – the writings of Scripture, *the Old Testament*. They searched the bible of the day. These Bereans were more noble in their exercise of study, with their ability to study, that they were able to search the Hebrew and Aramaic Scriptures in their Greek translation of the day. If they were in synagogue, as they were, it may be likely that they had not only the Greek Old Testament, but also the Hebrew Old Testament Scriptures, at least *some* scrolls.

When did they do this? They did it "daily." *Each day.* The expression "daily" can be specific, *every day*, or even used as in the general use of the word, *daily.* Luke observes that they searched the Scriptures every day as Paul taught them.

Why did they do this? "... to find out whether these things were so." They searched the Old Testament to see if what Paul was saying about *the Gospel* was true. They looked in the Old Testament to discern the truth of the Gospel; to consequently discern the manner of these spiritual truths.[3] Speaking of these certain Bereans, which received the word of God with love, Luke calls them "more noble men than the rest," (Acts 17:11), which shows very clearly that God counts men noble who have a noble spirit. When they heard the Apostle Paul preach, he being the great doctor of the Gentiles, the chief teacher of his time, they brought his doctrine to the test, trying and examining whether those things which were spoken and delivered by him were true. Were they agreeable to the doctrine found in Moses and the Prophets, that doctrine which they had already received?

What does Luke record in the text concerning the truth of Paul's words? "Therefore, many of them believed, and also not a few of the Greeks, prominent women as well as men," (Acts 17:11-12). The outcome of this zealous daily search, was *salvation*. They could not have rightly done this without having been in some ways predisposed to the material presented. They were in the synagogue. They were willing to hear Paul. They then rightly applied what they heard to be sure that such teachings lined up in accordance *to the word.* I would imagine at this point these Bereans would have needed to revamp their theology. They would have had to rethink everything they had learned about the Old

---

[3] "They then that can find no Gospel in the Old Testament, sufficiently bewray their ignorance both of the Old Testament and the New." Roberts, Francis, *Mysterium & Medulla Bibliorum, the Mysterie and Marrow of the Bible*, (London: R.W. for George Calvert, 1657) 637.

Testament and start over since Jesus Christ had now come, and they needed to apply these "new" thoughts to the "old" testament Scriptures. All that they thought, or how they thought, needed to be turned upside down on itself, and they needed a diligent search to prove out what Paul was saying by the power of the Holy Spirit; for the world is turned upside down by such theology. They needed to rightly align their understanding with the intent of the Holy Spirit in Scripture in the Old Testament.[4] And is this not the great aim of the minister to connect the mind of the people to the mind and intention of the Holy Spirit in the inscripturated word? To rightly understand prophetic fulfillment, and what it was that Paul was teaching concerning the Messiah who came, died, rose again, ascended, and presently intercedes in heaven, they had to read, examine and study, and discern this teaching out of the Old Testament. As a result of successfully doing this, many were converted, many were saved and many believed.

DOCTRINE: It is a Christian duty to daily and zealously read and study the Scriptures for salvation and spiritual profit.

Allow me to make a first note. Having the ability of reading the bible does not take away either preaching, or pastoral direction, or any other kind of ministerial help necessary to understanding the word of God.

---

[4] "There is much Gospel in the Old Testament; the comforts of the Gospel in the New Testament have their rise from the Old." Watson, Thomas. *A Body of Practical Divinity* (London: Printed for Thomas Parkurst, 1692) 16.

Consider that these Bereans did not engage in something new, but took it upon themselves to discern the apostle's teaching. Having a bible does not do away with ministers, but rather, it *confirms* their office. There is no "me and my bible alone." Christians are never islands to themselves. These students of Scripture were in the synagogue meeting together to study Scripture in light of what the rabbis taught. With that said, the daily reading and study of the Scriptures is commanded by Christ throughout the entire Bible.

Read the bible. The command of God to read the bible daily applies to all men for all time. "You shall love the LORD your God with all your heart, with all your soul, and with all your strength." How is this done? "And these words which I command you today shall be in your heart. You shall teach them diligently to your children, and shall talk of them when you sit in your house, when you walk by the way, when you lie down, and when you rise up," (Deut. 6:5-8). The Scriptures are signposts to those committed to God and true religion.[5] "This Book

---

[5] Basil saw them in the following manner, "When he had read the Bible over, he says, that it is a physician's shop of preservatives, against poisoned heresies. A pattern of profitable laws, against rebellions spirits; a treasury of most costly jewels, against beggarly rudiments; a foundation of most pure water springing up unto everlasting life. The origin thereof being from heaven, not from earth; the Author being God, not man, the matter verity, piety; purity, uprightness. The form is God's word, Gods testimony, Gods oracles are effects, light of understanding, repentance from dead works, newness of life, peace and holiness the end and reward of the study." Lupton, D. *The Glory of Their Times,* (London: I. Okes, 1640) 230-231.

of the Law shall not depart from your mouth, but you shall meditate in it day and night, that you may observe to do according to all that is written in it. For then you will make your way prosperous, and then you will have good success," (Joshua 1:8). Is God serious in this? Day and night? He is as serious as a heart attack.[6] The constant nature of submission to the word and will of God in reading and study is *daily*. "Blessed is he who reads and those who hear the words of this prophecy, and keeps those things which are written in it," (Rev. 1:3). Reads, hears, and keeps. When? Sometimes? Once a week? Once a month? Only when one feels like it? Such people who read the word, hear the word and keep the word, are in a class of *nobility*. They are and become blessed and more blessed.[7] They are singled out by the Holy Spirit as those blessed in such an action.

People sometimes say, "I don't think such and such a doctrine is essential to the Christian faith." If it's found in the word, the Lord wrote it down for men to read it, know it, study and teach it and speak constantly about it, and regardless where one thinks it is important or not, all the word of God is *the word of God*.[8] God's

---

[6] "... they must addict themselves to read the Bible." Vaughan, W. *Approved Directions for Health*, (London: T. Snodham for Roger Jackson, 1612), 70.

[7] "Blessed are the undefiled in the way, who walk in the law of the LORD," (Psa. 119:1). "But be ye doers of the word, and not hearers only, deceiving your own selves," (James 1:22). "But he said, Yea rather, blessed are they that hear the word of God, and keep it," (Luke 11:28).

[8] "Thy word have I hid in mine heart, that I might not sin against thee," (Psa. 119:11).

description of the Christian relies heavily on whether they believe what Scripture says, whether the doctrine is hard to understand or whether it is easy for them.

The Scriptures were given for the profit and salvation of God's people. "And it shall be with him, and he shall read therein all the days of his life: that he may learn to fear the LORD his God, to keep all the words of this law and these statutes, to do them," (Deut. 17:19). Christians are to be equipped through the word of God. "All Scripture is given by inspiration of God, and is profitable for doctrine, for reproof, for correction, for instruction in righteousness, that the man of God may be complete, thoroughly equipped for every good work," (2 Tim. 3:16-17). *The 1647 Westminster Larger Catechism* in question 157 asks, "How is the word of God to be read? Answer: The holy scriptures are to be read with an high and reverent esteem of them; with a firm persuasion that they are the very word of God, and that he only can enable us to understand them; with desire to know, believe, and obey the will of God revealed in them; with diligence, and attention to the matter and scope of them; with meditation, application, self-denial, and prayer." The word of God is to be read, and understood *daily.*

What does it mean to *profit* by something? In this case of daily reading and study it means to gain from reading and study what God intended for real sanctifying ends. It means people learn from the word. It means people are converted by the word. It means the saints are equipped for service by the word. It means all the spiritual comforts of the people of God are found in it.[9] It does this in an informative and in a corrective manner. It exposes sin,[10] mortifies it,[11] sanctifies the soul,[12] and conforms the soul to Jesus Christ.[13] It demonstrates man's need of God.[14] It shows man's miserable estate. It shows the burden of the Law. It shows the rest that the sinners[15] can find in Jesus Christ,[16] God's Messiah,[17] through the Gospel.[18]

Bible reading fuels all Christian duty including the importance of personal, private devotions. Without

---

[9] "Comfort your hearts, and stablish you in every good word and work," (2 Thess. 2:17). "Let, I pray thee, thy merciful kindness be for my comfort, according to thy word unto thy servant," (Psa. 119:76).

[10] "That he might sanctify and cleanse it with the washing of water by the word," (Eph. 5:26).

[11] "...strengthen thou me according unto thy word," (Psa. 119:28).

[12] "The law of the LORD is perfect, converting the soul: the testimony of the LORD is sure, making wise the simple," (Psa. 19:7).

[13] "...be ye transformed by the renewing of your mind, that ye may prove what is that good, and acceptable, and perfect, will of God," (Rom. 12:2).

[14] "And Jesus answered him, saying, It is written, That man shall not live by bread alone, but by every word of God," (Luke 4:4). "Because he hath despised the word of the LORD, and hath broken his commandment, that soul shall utterly be cut off; his iniquity shall be upon him," (Num. 15:31).

[15] "...quicken thou me according to thy word," (Psa. 119:25).

[16] "...heard the word of the Lord Jesus," (Acts 19:10).

[17] "The Spirit of the Lord GOD is upon me; because the LORD hath anointed me to preach good tidings unto the meek; he hath sent me to bind up the brokenhearted, to proclaim liberty to the captives, and the opening of the prison to them that are bound," (Isa. 61:1).

[18] "For the word of God is quick, and powerful, and sharper than any two edged sword, piercing even to the dividing asunder of soul and spirit, and of the joints and marrow, and is a discerner of the thoughts and intents of the heart," (Heb. 4:12).

reading the bible, Christians can never pray. They must first know *how* to pray. They must next know *to whom* to pray. They must next know *about* whom it is they pray to. They must next know what makes for a powerful prayer, in comparison to hypocrisy or babbling. They must know the content of prayer. What makes prayer a prayer rather than talking? There is a great difference between talking at God and praying to God. The Bible demonstrates these differences.

Without reading the Bible, Christians cannot meditate on the word. If they do not know the content of Scripture they can never know the harmony of Scripture. They cannot know the harmony of Scripture unless they have *read* it all. How could they possibly say they know what God says about life and godliness if they have never read all their bible? The best answer such a one could give is "I don't know the answer to that yet until I've read all my bible." It would be like trying to discern a billboard on the other side of a forest, through all the trees. Such a thing is nearly impossible. They may rely far too much on people coming out of the forest telling them what they think the billboard says, without ever seeing it in full themselves. No wonder why Evangelical Christians, polled over the last two decades, show that only 8% of the church read their whole bible more than one time in their Christian walk. They cannot understand Scripture's unity unless they understand its content. They cannot fulfill any commanded directive to meditate on God's word day and night, if they are unfamiliar with it. Some Christians think that once they have read whatever they consider enough of the Bible, they are *done.* There are even bibles published today that contain the New Testament and Psalms, deleting 3/4ths of the inscripturated word, which is a very odd practice for professing believers who love God and his word. There are even many so-called teachers and pastors today who say that the Old Testament is no longer needed for the New Testament church. *Tell that* to the studied Bereans who studied the Scriptures daily and were converted, meaning *the Old Testament.* When Paul said all Scripture is God-breathed,[19] he was speaking directly about the Old Testament, for there was no New Testament yet.

Without reading the bible, fathers cannot teach their families or their children.[20] What shall they teach them if not the word of God? Where will they find what to teach them? What will be the content of transforming spiritual power for their family if not in the word.

If Christians would profit from reading the Bible, they must prepare their hearts for reading the word. 1 Samuel 7:3 says, "Prepare your hearts to the Lord." Many come rashly to their personal devotions. It is no wonder

---

[19] "All scripture is given by inspiration of God, and is profitable for doctrine, for reproof, for correction, for instruction in righteousness," (2 Tim. 3:16). Paul was speaking immediately about the Old Testament but mediately about the New Testament by way of the Spirit's work of carrying him as he wrote.

[20] "Now therefore hearken, O Israel, unto the statutes and unto the judgments, which I teach you, for to do them, that ye may live," (Deut. 4:1).

that if they come without preparation, they go away without profit.[21] They must have a plan and many times they must diligently labor to understand what they read. No, they may not have classical training like those noble Bereans who became more noble in their studies being brought up in well-to-do families. But they can pray as the psalmist, Psalm 119:73, "Give me understanding, that I may learn your commandments." Who provides this cure? Why, the Holy Spirit and his power of *spiritual persuasion.* Make note of that phrase, but for now, keep that tucked away in the back of your mind for a moment. Though there are some knots in Scripture which are not easily untied, yet, the Holy Spirit has plainly pointed out things essential to salvation and the Christian's sanctification in the word. Not everyone is a scholar or pastor. This is why Christ commissioned those skilled in the word to teach. However, the essentials for Christian salvation and living may be understood in an elementary manner.[22] The Lord Jesus even promises not to quench the smoking flax or break the bruised reed of

---

[21] "Many come rashly to the reading of the word; and no wonder, if they come without preparation, [that] they go away without profit." Nichols, J. *Puritan Sermons*, Volume 2, (Wheaton, IL: Richard Owen Roberts, Publishers, 1981) 60.

[22] "The scriptures are written so that plain and private men may get this light and spiritual understanding by them. Ps. 19:7, "The law of the Lord is perfect, converting the soul: the testimony of the Lord is sure, making wise the simple."" Manton, Thomas *The Complete Works of Thomas Manton*, Volume 8, (Worthington, IL: Maranatha Publications, 1979) 354.

this kind.[23] But for the depiction of nobility as the Spirit would testify of these Bereans, it is impossible to gain that rank without being familiar with *all the Scriptures*. Or, to not have spent time in diligent examination of them.

This is a serious business to read the word of God. Deut. 32:47 says that the Bible is life, "It is not a vain thing for you; *it is your life.*" These commands, statutes, judgments, promises and directives are life in contrast to death. They are promises in contrast to curses. Christians ought to believe that God's condescension in *covenant* to save, the love of Christ which caused him to die upon the cross, all these weighty matters of eternity, heaven, hell and the like, are very *serious* subjects.[24] It is no wonder why the there is no Scriptural joke book, of light jesting found anywhere in it.

Christ has loved mankind more than the angels that fell, (Heb. 2:7). Christ loved his people more than physical life itself. This is a love that passes knowledge; who can read this without seriousness? Do Christians see other Christians reading their Bible striving for heaven with agony, (Luke 13:24)? Scripture cautions people not to fall short of the promised rest, (Heb. 4:1).

---

[23] "A bruised reed shall he not break, and smoking flax shall he not quench, till he send forth judgment unto victory," (Matt. 12:20).

[24] "Take off your thoughts sometimes from the world, and compel them to dwell on serious subjects." Edwards, Jonathan, We Ought to Make Religion Our Present and Immediate Business. In W. H. Kimnach (Ed.), *Jonathan Edwards Sermons,* (New Haven, CT: The Jonathan Edwards Center at Yale University) electronic ed.

It describes the horrors of infernal torments in hell, with the worm of a bitter conscience, and the fire which never ceases, (Mark 9:44). Imagine setting out for heaven like Ignorance did in Bunyan's *Pilgrim's Progress* and making it all the way to the gate of the Celestial City only to find out that the mouth of hell was there as well? Who cannot take all this without being serious?

Christians ought to labor to remember what they read. The devil desires to steal the word out of their mind so that they can never make use of it. "Therefore behold, I am against the prophets," says the LORD, "who steal My words every one from his neighbor," (Jer. 23:30). Contrary to this, the Psalmist says in Psalm 119:52, "I remembered your judgments of old." How can one remember the judgments of old if they are unfamiliar with the judgments of old? Christians are to have, "the word dwell in us," (Col. 3:16). If the word does not ultimately stick in the memory, it cannot profit. There must be a daily exercise of reading and then study.

Reading the Bible daily differs from Bible *study.* "The works of the LORD are great, studied by all who have pleasure in them," (Psa. 111:2).[25] "And you shall teach them the statutes and the laws, and show them the way in which they must walk and the work they must

---

[25] This is a very interesting word, with many applications in Scripture in the Hebrew for the translation of "studied." Literally, in its root, it may be translated "inquire about," or "care about" someone or something. It also has connotations of specifically to *study* and *expound* as Ezra did in Ezra 7:10. It is something "worth investigating" and into that which the Christian is to "inquire."

do," (Exod. 18:20). How would they know this without knowing what God actually said? They would first have to read the Bible, before they could in turn teach the bible; even if teaching it to themselves. In the harmony of all its parts, it is to be understood, and if it is to be understood, it is to be familiar. "And that you may teach the children of Israel all the statutes which the LORD has spoken to them by the hand of Moses," (Lev. 10:11). How could the priests and Levites teach anything without knowing and understanding them thoroughly? Did they have theological books? Commentaries? No. Like the Bereans, they studied the word daily and became intimately familiar with it. It was said of John Bunyan that if you cut him he would bleed the bible. This is the idea.

"...but I will teach you the good and the right way," (1 Sam. 12:23). How would you know what the good and right way is without knowing both sides – the good way and the bad way? "Age should speak, and multitude of years should teach wisdom," (Job 32:7). If those with wisdom are to teach God's will and word, how can they have wisdom without having the right application of knowledge? They must *know*, in order to be *wise* to teach. "Show me Your ways, O LORD; Teach me Your paths. Lead me in Your truth and teach me, For You are the God of my salvation," (Psa. 25:4-5). Knowing the truth of Christ and God is predicated upon *knowing something*.

And all this reading and study and teaching in the family and church would prove to be unprofitable, if there were not something of God, Christ and redemption in it. The Reformation of the church never consists in bringing in new doctrines or new teachings. Rather, it is abiding in the old paths, in the word, the *Old Time Religion.* This takes time with readiness of spirit, eagerness and being fair minded. Nicholas Byfield, said, "Do not look at the profit you think you have only after a week or two. That is too short a time of making notes and asking questions. You must think about this type of reading and study over the course of a year, or two years or five years."[26] Reading and study take time.

You must have a strategy in reading and studying the Bible. First, let me give you a note of warning on this. Do not look for nobility for *the sake of* nobility. It is very true that the Holy Spirit calls some *noble* who read and study effectively. But, you are not in it for a title. You are in it to *draw near to Christ.*

Now, as much as it is important for you to read Scripture daily, at the same time, it can be overwhelming to figure out a strategy for reading. There are 66 books in the bible, divided into the Old and New Testaments, covering historical narrative, didactic teaching, poetry, prophesy, wisdom literature, epistles, *etc.* Each book varies in length. Jude is one chapter. Psalm 119 is one chapter but really the equivalent of 22 chapters. Mark's

---

[26] Byfield, Nicholas, *The Rules of a Holy Life*, (Crossville, TN: Puritan Publications, 2016) 111-112.

chapters are shorter overall, and Luke's chapters are longer overall. The book of Haggai is merely 2 chapters, where Isaiah is 66 chapters. There are books dealing with long genealogies, like Numbers, and those with apologetic purposes like Judges, which was written as an argument for the monarchy of the united holy nation. Some of Paul's letters are pastoral in nature, like 1 and 2 Timothy written to the young pastor, and others which are concerned with doctrine, like Romans. The Christian has much to consider when beginning to map out having a strategy for reading the Scriptures. But do not be dissuaded, you *must* have a strategy.

Consider reading 3 chapters each day. 2 chapters from the Old Testament and one from the New Testament. Why? There are 1189 chapters in the whole bible. There are 365 days in a year. That gives you as a reader 3 chapters a day, with a leftover chapter to read at the end of the year, to complete reading the entire bible in one year. You should read the bible *at least once every year.* And even when you do that, that strategy will only get you reading the bible 75 times if you live to be 90 or so. Is that really *enough?* An even better strategy is to read 6 chapters a day, which in turn will allow you to read the New Testament 3 times and the Old Testament 2 times every year. For the beginner, in just seeing the importance of this, stick with the *3 chapter strategy.*

You should begin reading the bible at the beginning. *God* started there. Read 1 chapter of Genesis, 1 chapter from the psalms, and one chapter of the Gospel of Matthew as you begin, and then continue from there. Once the New Testament is completed, read through the rest of the Old Testament to complete your year's reading.

Sometimes people complain that in bible reading they can't always read with comfort and profit. It's like a large book, or a little library to them. Don't get overwhelmed with reading by making *reading* too difficult. Reading is *not* study. Reading is *reading*. Differentiate the two. Take a highlighter and mark in your bible the verses, or phrases that pop out to you in your reading, that are meaningful. Each year (each time you complete your reading of the whole bible), change the color of the highlighter. That will even furnish you with verses to memorize from your reading, or verses to study.

In contrast to reading, I'm also going to give you seven steps to Bible *study*. Now this is *study*, not reading. From your reading you come across a verse that pops out at you. In study, it is here that you take some time to consider what *that* verse means. I would, however, say that this should only be done *after* one has a good familiarity with the Scriptures overall. In other words, read the whole bible first, then implement study of the bible after you have read it through.

Consider these seven steps. First, (as I told you to hold that thought on the Spirit and his enlightenment) pray for the help of the Holy Spirit. I'll spend a moment on this in general being as important as it is. Jesus said, "Without me you can do nothing."[27] You cannot read, you cannot pray, you cannot worship, you cannot please the Lord *in any way*, no you cannot read or study the Bible without his help. Fruitfulness is dependent on him. It is *his* fruit. It is a Bible about him and from him. Contrasted in Galatians 5 is your fruit,[28] and the Spirit's fruit.[29] Your fruit is all sin. The Spirit's fruit through you is the love of study, joy in study, peace from study, patience in study, seeing God's kindness in sanctifying you through study, the good that comes out of study, increased faith in study, humility in study and all-around sanctification, (Gal. 5:19-23). You must take Christ along with you, and this is done through the help of the power of the Holy Spirit.

Spiritual blindness is opposite to divine illumination. One who is spiritually blind cannot understand Scripture as God intends. "But the natural man does not receive the things of the Spirit of God, for they are foolishness to him; nor can he know them, because they are spiritually discerned," (1 Cor. 2:14). You must be regenerate first, believe what you have read

---

[27] John 15:5.

[28] "Now the works of the flesh are manifest, which are these; Adultery, fornication, uncleanness, lasciviousness, idolatry, witchcraft, hatred, variance, emulations, wrath, strife, seditions, heresies, envyings, murders, drunkenness, revellings, and such like: of the which I tell you before, as I have also told you in time past, that they which do such things shall not inherit the kingdom of God," (Gal. 5:19-21).

[29] "But the fruit of the Spirit is love, joy, peace, longsuffering, gentleness, goodness, faith, meekness, temperance: against such there is no law," (Gal. 5:22-23).

second, and grow by the word third. "But the wisdom that is from above is first pure, then peaceable, gentle, willing to yield, full of mercy and good fruits, without partiality and without hypocrisy," (James 3:17). There is a special knowledge of divine mysteries formed in us by the special and sanctifying work of the Holy Spirit. Wisdom comes from above because it is of God. "And they shall all be taught by God," (John 6:45). Divine illumination comes from Christ and the intercession he gives on behalf of his saints in the work of the Spirit sent from his throne to you when you are born again. It is necessary from the Spirit because the substance of what is read is of the highest spiritual nature. These are not trivial things, and must be rightly discerned. William Spurstowe a Westminster Divine said, "divine illumination and teachings of the Spirit, both enlightens the mind and inclines the will to choose the one thing which is necessary."[30] All this is summed up in this one important verse: "Open my eyes, that I may see wondrous things from Your law," (Psa. 119:18). Once you are enlightened by the Spirit at your regeneration, you continue to pray for the Spirit's testimony to the truth of the word in your heart as you read it. I call this "spiritual persuasion." It is set in the context of *prayer.* It is set in the realization that wonderous things will never be known without his spiritual help. The psalmist

---

[30] Spurstowe, William, *The Spiritual Chemyst, or Divine Meditations on Several Subjects*, (Coconut Creek: Puritan Publications, 2012) Meditation #25.

here doesn't ask God to give him a new book that is simpler to understand, but rather, that, he see more clearly. But seeing involves knowing and perceiving the truth. And perceiving and knowing the truth is by study of the word. Do not expect the Holy Spirit to "zap" you when you read a passage as if knowledge comes without study. Most people that have read about the Spirit's divine illumination think that Christ, through the Spirit, zaps them instantaneously as if they will suddenly be experts on a passage without taking time to study it. The Spirit spiritually persuades you as you understand what the text *says* and what the text *means*. That means you have to *study* the bible.[31]

Second, don't give God your dopey time. What is "dopey time?" Some of you have a better study time at 6am than others. Some like to study at night, at midnight. Choose the best time. If you are falling asleep, or can't concentrate, this would be considered your "dopey time." That time needs to be reserved for something other than handling God's word carefully and diligently striving towards nobility. If you find that you have fallen behind in your reading and study, the Lord's Day is a good time for catching up, is a great time to

---

[31] "We may read the Bible over, but we cannot learn to purpose, till the Spirit of God shine into our hearts. Oh, implore this blessed Spirit, it is God's royal prerogative to teach, "I am the Lord thy God, that teacheth thee to profit." Watson, Thomas, (1654). *Autarkeia, or, The Art of Divine Contentment*, (London: T.M. for Ralph Smith, 1654) 19.

immerse yourself in the word.[32] Put down your work and pick up God's work.

Third, don't rush your study. Fix your mind on the subject at hand. It would be a waste of time to try and fool yourself in "pretending to study" while you are thinking about chores around the house or having to mow the lawn later on. Have solitude, concentrate and take your time.

Fourth, be sure to choose a place of study (and consequently of devotions) that is quiet and away from distractions. This seems simple, but for busy moms and dads, this is not as easily done as one would think. Plan that out accordingly, and to the best of your ability.

Fifth, when you start your study, direct your mind to improve a single thought on a single verse or idea. You are looking for clarity on a particular point, to see it more clearly. Don't leave that point until you are its master.[33] View it in every light that you can with cross referencing other Scriptures. Endeavor to discern how many ways you can express it in the shortest and best manner so that it can be mentally retained. This requires you to be a good student, which means a good exegete of Scripture, one who can rightly apply the skills

---

[32] Herbert Palmer said, "Neglect not thy usual personal devotions, but rather enlarge them," on the Lord's Day. *Memorials of Godliness & Christianity* (London: Printed for Henry Million, 1670) 118.

[33] "For precept must be upon precept, precept upon precept; line upon line, line upon line; here a little, and there a little," (Isa. 28:10).

of hermeneutics. If you are not skilled in hermeneutics, consider making *that study* a priority.[34]

Sixthly, have patience. "... imitate those who through faith and patience inherit the promises," (Heb. 6:12). This is a fruit of the Spirit. The more you familiarize yourself to laborious thinking in studying the bible, the better you will be able to abide in it. And don't be afraid of gaining help from solid, godly books later on after being familiar with reading all your Bible, that will guide you in each study you take on.

Seventh, memorize Scripture. "Your word have I hid in my heart, that I might not sin against you," (Psa. 119:11). Reading gains familiarity. Study gains insight. Memorization gains weapons.[35] Memorize your highlighted verses from your bible reading. Make a strategy of it. By Luther's older age, he had memorized most of the bible. Choose a version that suits your capacity that is at least faithful to its translation and stick with that. What does it do to your heart when the bible is in your head? *Try it and see.*

Profiting in Bible reading and study is of utmost importance. "Therefore lay aside all filthiness and overflow of wickedness, and receive with meekness the

---

[34] See my workbook on the *Reformed Apprentice Series* to help in that area.

[35] "O the miserable defect of knowledge, even among Professors themselves, for want of humility and diligence to commit to memory the principles of religion?" Alleine, Joseph. (1674). *A Most Familiar Explanation of the Assemblies Shorter Catechism,* An Admonition to the Reader, (London: Printed for Edw. Brewster, 1674) electronic ed.

implanted word, which is able to save your souls," (James 1:21). James gives an important directive which is the reception of the word of God at the expense of sin. This verse comes just before James 1:23 which tells them to be *doers* of the word, not just *hearers*. They are not simply to have the word threaded through their eyes, or ears. There must be more to it than that. There is no attentive hearing, no attentive reading, no attentive study of the word if sin lies dominant in your heart. The unconverted in this find such study a great burden, and it is, until they come to Christ for rest. The distracted Christian finds such reading and study as a burden, and it is, until those distractions are put off and away. James instructs to receive the word with meekness, which means the student cannot be angry with what the word says or what God directs you to understand about his beloved Son. How many times could we find wicked kings or prideful Pharisees who scoffed at what God's ministers taught? "I don't like what it says, so I'm going to believe what I want." That's Pharaoh, "Who is the Lord that I should obey his voice and let Israel go?"[36]

If you are diligent and zealous to profit in bible reading and study, God *will* describe you as noble by application. As it stands today, if the Spirit of God were to write a memoir about you, how would he describe your Christian devotion to reading and studying the Bible? Drowsy, lazy, wandering, inattentive; *or noble?* The Bereans were inscripturated by the Spirit of God as

---

[36] Eph. 5:2.

noble students of the word. Understand that your heart is a battle ground for the word. The devil is after those who would hear God communicate to them about his Son. He knows that the word of God is all about Jesus Christ and enlivens a Christian's desire to commune with God more and more.[37]

I leave you with this quote by the puritan Thomas Senior who said, "Pray to the Lord, that he would preserve the word in your hearts by his Spirit.— The devil would snatch away the word of God from us, if there were not a stronger to guard it, and that is the Holy Spirit: "That good thing which was committed to thee keep, by the Holy Ghost which dwelleth in us." (2 Tim. 1:14.) Pray then after the word, as David: "O Lord God of Abraham, Isaac, and Israel, our fathers, keep this for ever in the imagination of the thoughts of the hearts of thy people." (1 Chron. 29:18) And such a prayer, coming from an honest heart, shall secure the word, so that it shall abide with you, and it shall come after to your minds; it shall come seasonably in the very nick and stress of necessity, and it shall come with effectiveness and power."[38] Yet all of this is for naught, if we are unfamiliar with the word.

---

[37] "And beginning at Moses and all the prophets, he expounded unto them in all the scriptures the things concerning himself," (Luke 24:27).
[38] Senior, Thomas, Sermon: How may the duty of daily family prayer be best managed for the spiritual benefit of every one in the family? Editor, Nichols, James, *Puritan Sermons*, Volume 2, (Wheaton, IL: Richard Owen Roberts, Publishers, 1981) 57.

Mark 2: Daily Meditation

"Blessed is the man that walketh not in the counsel of the ungodly, nor standeth in the way of sinners, nor sitteth in the seat of the scornful. But his delight is in the law of the LORD; and in his law doth he meditate day and night. And he shall be like a tree planted by the rivers of water, that bringeth forth his fruit in his season; his leaf also shall not wither; and whatsoever he doeth shall prosper," (Psa. 1:1-3).

Psalm 1 is the beginning of the Psalter, the Book of praises. God's aim and chief end is his glory, and his praise. What more suitable book in Scripture is there than a whole compendium of praises to give the Lord? This first psalm can be seen as an introduction to the psalter as a whole. St. Jerome called it the "the preface of the Holy Spirit" to the Psalms. It outlines, in reality, the portrait of a godly man. The psalms as a whole outline *the godly saint*, and are often referred to by many good theologians as a "little bible." Everything of God and Christ, of holiness and Spirit-power, of walking and living before God is found in the psalter.[1]

---

[1] "If we consider how many mysteries of religion are opened to us in the Psalter, how many things concerning Christ, what clear [predictions] concerning his birth, his priesthood, his kingdom, his death, the very circumstances of his passion, his resurrection, and all the degrees of his exaltation-more clearly and explicitly recorded in the Psalter, then in all the old Prophets besides, we may easily believe that Christ with a *Key of David* in his hand, is nothing else but Christ fully opened and manifested to us in the Psalms in the

This first psalm is a teaching or wisdom psalm commanding the readers to devote themselves to the study of God's word, and, as all covenant concepts flow, it gives warnings if these directives are neglected. It shows forth *both* blessings and curses.

The psalm consists of two sections. The first section deals with verses 1–3 which describe the godly person, showing what he refuses, what he does and then a description of him as a healthy tree. The second section with verses 4–6, compares the wicked to chaff, which is blown away by the wind. The wicked will not endure, and they will not experience the delight and happiness of the saints. They will in fact be crushed in the judgment, and they will be destined to eternal destruction in hell under God's wrath, from which there will be no escape.

One might title this psalm, "the way to true happiness."[2] It is a commentary and direction on the perfect way and the good path that people take to be happy. All people, for all time, desire to be *happy*. Life, liberty and the pursuit of happiness is the American motto and bound up in the Declaration of Independence,

---

whole mystery of our redemption." Taylor, Jeremy, *The Psalter of David with Titles ... whereunto is added Devotions for the help and assistance of all Christian people, in all occasions and necessities,* (London: Printed for R. Royston, 1647) electronic ed.

[2] This psalm, as with all others, "being embraced and known, they make a man happy, Psalm 119:97-98; Luke 10:42, 16:29; Psalm 1:2; Rev. 1:3, because, when the Scriptures are neglected, or condemned, they plunge men into all misery, Heb. 2:3; Matt. 22:29; Psalm 50:16." Dickson, David, *Truths Victory Over Error,* (Edinburgh: John Reid, 1684) 17.

"We hold these truths to be self-evident: that all men are created equal; that they are endowed by their Creator with certain unalienable rights; that among these are life, liberty, and the pursuit of happiness." Where will people find this happiness?

The first three verses start with "Blessed is the man." *Blessed* is translated in light of the way to true happiness. *Happy.* Are you happy? Who does not want to be happy? Who does not want a full life? Who does not want their life to *mean something* in the end? What is the redemptive value in the Kingdom of God for *that* person? Blessings, in this psalm, are both external and internal. Blessings come from God alone, and are dispensed by God. People say all the time, "We are so blessed." They often think that material blessing is what constitutes blessings. Things like health, a fine family, lots of money, fame, honors, status and the like. In the Psalm, God directs the reader to consider where being blessed originates from. Make note, the psalm does not say that he is *a good man.* There is no one good no not one.[3] It says he is a *blessed* man. This kind of blessing is far different than what one might hear from their neighbor who was blessed just the other day, or people in their workplace who are blessed because they found their keys under the sofa. The psalm instructs that

---

[3] "They are all gone aside, they are all together become filthy: there is none that doeth good, no, not one," (Psa. 14:3). Compare Romans 3:12.

Christians simply do not have "blessings" but they are blessed by God in a *most specific manner.*

"Who walks not in the counsel of the ungodly, nor stands in the path of sinners, nor sits in the seat of the scornful." This blessed man does not walk, stand or sit in unlawful ways. The blessed man is a spiritual man. He does not move in action, he does not remain in the company of, or, make his resting place the companionship of the wicked. There is a discernable separation between the blessed person and the world, *i.e.* those who "hang out with" worldly people. It is against the character and quality of a blessed and godly man to accompany the wicked in any way, according to this psalm. They do not take the path of sinners. They do not contemplate the direction of the wicked. They do not make the ungodly their company. Ungodly people are those who scorn God, scoff at him, those who wag their fingers and gnash their teeth at God in three ways: by actively or passively disregarding what God commands them to do, by doing what their own selfish desires are – even if it is a good thing done in a godless way. By directly scoffing against God. The godly man has nothing to do with those opposed to true religion. He rejects, in every form, all kinds of atheism, although, this psalm will indeed show whether one is a blessed man or not merely by his actions. This *avoidance* of evil is not enough to bring the godly man to heaven. It is really coming down to the difference between crying out against sin and abhorring sin in the heart. Men may cry

41

out against some sin who have never experienced hating sin in their heart. Some say, "Don't be cruel to animals." Some say, "Save the trees." Others say, "Be neighborly." All these, and more, are crying out against their perception of sin, but such people may have never experience *abhorring sin* because they have never been changed by God.

Many times, people, in some legal manner, try to make themselves look good by simply running on these negatives. They are not as other men are. They are not cheaters. They are not liars. They are not drunkards. They are not profaning the Lord's Day. They are not associating with such and such people who do all manner of wickedness. Legal performances in this way are not enough.[4] The godly man is not only described in this negative manner of *not* being like this, but he is also described in a positive manner of being *like* something else. Avoiding evil is a good thing.[5] But it is not the only thing, and it is never enough. A wicked man can't avoid this anyway. Even if a wicked man cries out against all manner of sin and injustice, his *heart* still is bad.[6] He has

---

[4] The claim "that they are not as other men, intemperate, debauched, drunkards, revelers, and the like; while at the same time they look upon fraud and deceit, tricking and over-reaching, as the necessary art and mystery of business." Clarke, Samuel, *Three Practical Essays ... containing instructions for a holy life*, (London: Printed for James Knapton, 1699) 197.

[5] "Enter not into the path of the wicked, and go not in the way of evil men. Avoid it, pass not by it, turn from it, and pass away," (Prov. 4:14-15).

[6] "That no natural or unregenerate man is able to do any thing, though never so little that is good, because he is a bad Tree, and

a bad record because of Adam's sin which is credited to his account making him a sinner.[7] A man's outward avoidance of sin does not mean he is a blessed man, or blessed of God. What shows that he is blessed?

"But his delight is in the law of the LORD." The Law of God is used as a metaphor for the word of God.[8] It must be a truly great spiritual discipline for the saints to delight in this, and to be blessed as a result. For the saints, to love something attached to the Lord Jesus Christ is that which drives them into delight. The saints delight is God's word because the word shows them more plainly who Jesus is.[9] For a Christian, their whole life is about knowing Christ more.[10] For the non-Christian, they are happy when they know Christ *less.*[11]

Whatever the saint loves, this is how he thinks.

---

being also of the seed of Serpents, there cannot come any honey, or sweet thing from him." Burgess, *Original Sin*, 102.

[7] "... as by one man sin entered into the world, and death by sin; and so death passed upon all men, for that all have sinned," (Rom. 5:12).

[8] "But now the righteousness of God without the law is manifested, being witnessed by the law and the prophets," (Rom. 3:21). "The law and the prophets were until John: since that time the kingdom of God is preached, and every man presseth into it," (Luke 16:16). "On these two commandments hang all the law and the prophets," (Matt. 22:40).

[9] "The word which God sent unto the children of Israel, preaching peace by Jesus Christ: (he is Lord of all)," (Acts 10:36).

[10] "That their hearts might be comforted, being knit together in love, and unto all riches of the full assurance of understanding, to the acknowledgement of the mystery of God, and of the Father, and of Christ; In whom are hid all the treasures of wisdom and knowledge," (Col. 2:2-3).

[11] "The wicked, through the pride of his countenance, will not seek after God: God is not in all his thoughts," (Psa. 10:4).

The godly take "delight" in the word of God. "I delight to do thy will, O my God: yea, thy law is within my heart," (Psa. 40:8).[12] It is not only in seeing its content, but delight concerns obeying the word of God as much as it does understanding it.[13]

If the blessed man delights in God's word, then, there is nothing that will hinder him from it. He is not too tired. He is not too busy. He is not going to use the excuse that he is incapable of study or understanding. Such a man gives his *best* to God, and his delight for the word of God and godliness is his chief aim and position.[14] He does not delight so much in worldly things.[15] Things of the world are empty to him in comparison to the Savior.[16] His mind is, in fact, set on the things above where Christ is seated at the right hand of God.[17] What does he do to engage himself in this delight, to the ultimate end of glorifying God in the way of true happiness?

---

[12] Consider, "but I delight in thy law," (Psa. 119:70). "I have longed for thy salvation, O LORD; and thy law is my delight," (Psa. 119:174). "For I delight in the law of God after the inward man," (Rom. 7:22).
[13] "And I will delight myself in thy commandments, which I have loved," (Psa. 119:47).
[14] "Thy testimonies also are my delight and my counsellors," (Psa. 119:24).
[15] "Teaching us that, denying ungodliness and worldly lusts, we should live soberly, righteously, and godly, in this present world; Looking for that blessed hope, and the glorious appearing of the great God and our Saviour Jesus Christ," (Titus 2:12-13).
[16] "Whose end is destruction, whose God is their belly, and whose glory is in their shame, who mind earthly things," (Phil. 3:19).
[17] "Set your affection on things above, not on things on the earth," (Col. 3:2).

"And in his law he meditates day and night." The godly man is described in two ways – he delights in the word,[18] and he meditates on the word. *Meditates* means he "pours over" or "thinks about it intensely". The Hebrew verb הָגָה *hagah* is defined as "reads carefully," "studies," "thinks about" meaning intensive, careful reading and study. Hear Gods commentary on such thinking, "This Book of the Law shall not depart from your mouth, but you shall meditate in it day and night, that you may observe to do according to all that is written in it. For then you will make your way prosperous, and then you will have good success," (Joshua 1:8).

One might say, "This psalm cannot possibly be *that* serious: meditating day and night?" Yes, God is very serious about what he says. The blessed man reads it and studies it day and night.[19] But, to satisfy the kicking back of that idea, it means that godly people *obsess* over God's word all the time in thinking about its application in all circumstances. They obsess over Christ, which means, they obsess over his word. He is, in fact, their Savior, and the Living Word. "In the beginning was the word, and the word was with God, and the word was God," (John

---

[18] "There are delights, variety of delights, in the word of God, which the saints have often the sweetest enjoyment." Henry, Matthew, *Matthew Henry's Commentary on the Whole Bible,* (Peabody: Hendrickson, 1994) 926.

[19] On this he thinks and meditates day and night, this is where his treasure is, and on it he sets his whole affection. He longs to enjoy it.

1:1). And so, "Unto you therefore which believe he is precious," (1 Peter 2:7).

And if the godly do this, they are given a description of the flourishing tree planted by rivers of flowing life-giving water. As the rivers of water flow out of those who are born again to eternal life in the Spirit. The psalmist is not merely meaning that a godly man will always be thinking on one topic, "the law of God". But that during the day he will use the word of God as a marker to point the way out of the paths of sinners, and onto a highway of holiness and happiness. During the night he will use it as a pillow on which to rest his mind. All of this is possible because he incessantly studies it because it is his delight.

"He shall be like a tree planted by the rivers of water, that brings forth its fruit in its season, whose leaf also shall not wither; And whatever he does shall prosper," (Psa. 1:1-3). Those godly people, looking for true happiness, who reject the way of the wicked, who spend their thinking about God's word and its application to them day and night, will be like a flourishing tree, that is always fruitful, and never dies, prospering in all their ways – the way of true happiness before God.[20]

DOCTRINE: It is the duty of Christians to meditate on the word of God day and night as the way

---

[20] "He that believeth on me, as the scripture hath said, out of his belly shall flow rivers of living water," (John 7:38). "... yea, happy is that people, whose God is the LORD," (Psa. 144:15).

to true happiness. Christians today think that meditating on the word of God is linked in some way to the New Age practice of transcendental meditation. Transcendental meditation is a technique made popular in yoga by the Indian guru Maharishi Mahesh Yogi (1911–2008), where we get the ancient Indian practice of "yoga" from (which means *union*). Yoga is a Hindu spiritual and ascetic discipline which includes breath control, meditation, and the adoption of specific bodily postures to connect spiritually with Brahman in *union*, the false Hindu concept of the supreme cosmic spirit. *Christians should have nothing to do with this.* This demonic practice concerns "detaching" one's self from their mind to promote harmony and self-realization by meditation (becoming one with the emptiness of the universe where one finds peace). This is done through the repetition of Hindu mantras or spells, and the practice of yoga postures; these are visible representations of *spiritual mantras* which are employed to contact demonic influences. This Satanic idea of meditation is not what biblical, godly meditation teaches in Scripture.

In contrast, biblical meditation is the exact opposite, looking to *fill up the mind* with high thoughts concerning Jesus Christ from Scripture to the glory of God.[21] Biblical meditation causes the Christian to have thoughtful daily studies of heavenly truths. This differs from both bible reading and bible study. Meditation on

---

[21] "...be ye transformed by the renewing of your mind," (Rom. 12:2).

Scripture is much different. If God is speaking to the Christian in the word of God, the Christian must first read what is there, then study to be sure they have the right interpretation or meaning behind what the Holy Spirit intended to tell them, and *then* they must meditate on it to make it useful to them. The bible in this way, is, in fact, God speaking to them. Meditation may be likened to the Christian's personal application of the word to their soul; like the applicatory part of a sermon that is applying a given text to the congregation.[22] In this case, the work is personal and applies the idea which is being meditated upon, to the personal soul in a time of set devotion.

It is not my intention to give you a full orbed view of godly meditation, broken down into various parts. That would be better served in a book all its own on the subject.[23] The intention here is to understand the Christian's basic duty in this, as a means of grace and as commanded by God, "And on his law he meditates day and night." The word of God in this way should be a constant companion to the believer.

---

[22] "What works of God we are particularly called to consider: his doings towards the children of men. Those works of God that concern ourselves, and that therefore we are especially concerned to consider and meditate on." Edwards, Jonathan, God's Glory in His Terribleness. In W. H. Kimnach (Ed.), *Jonathan Edwards Sermons,* (New Haven, CT: The Jonathan Edwards Center at Yale University, 2006) electronic ed.

[23] Puritan Publications has published a number of works on godly meditation.

Meditation is a serious solemn thinking of the things of God, to the end that Christians might understand how much God's word concerns them, and that their hearts by it may be raised to some holy affections and resolutions. It is a serious, earnest and purposed thinking on some point of Christian instruction, tending to lead a Christian forward toward the Kingdom of heaven, and serving for their daily strengthening against the flesh, the world and the devil that they may ultimately glorify and glory in Jesus Christ.[24]

Meditation is not bible study, and it is not bible reading. Again, for all intents and purposes, meditation is the *application portion* of a sermon. When Christians deal with the subject of divine meditation, this concerns the manner in which they are to be eternally happy, which means working a point of truth into the soul. It is a fundamental practical action which results in application of the word. When Christians study, the end of study is to have knowledge of some kind on a particular verse or passage. But, when Christians *meditate* on the word of God, the end of meditation is sanctification, *i.e.* that the Christian is changed in some way as a result. They make take a whole week, for example, and have a series of meditations on "godly duties to perform before God," which leads them to be a better Christian who is higher in religion by the end of

---

[24] Gen. 24:63; Joshua 1:8; Psalm 1:2, 5:1, 19:14, 49:3, 63:6, 77:12, 104:34, 119:15, 23, 48, 78, 97, 99, 148, 143:5; Isa. 33:18; 1 Tim. 4:15.

the week than they were the week before. In this, they work the word of God into their soul by the spiritual persuasion of the Spirit working alongside them to testify to the truth of the Scripture, that such a truth is applicable to them, and applies directly to them in Christ.

Scripture is filled with godly people meditating on the things of God. "And Isaac went out to meditate in the field in the evening," (Gen. 24:63). "I will meditate on all Your work," (Psalm 77:12). The word of God and the works of God must be the godly man's meditation. "Meditate on these things," (1 Timothy 4:15). Here in Timothy, and, by way of proportion, on every person, is meditation commanded.

There are two kinds of biblical meditation. There is occasional meditation, where the mind darts up to heaven to consider something that pops into the thoughts. A person may be in their garden, they are tending it, and they have a vine of squash, and they consider the life-giving sap of the True Vine, Jesus, that gives life to them. They consider some earthly idea and consider it in a spiritual manner. As Solomon directs, "Go to the ant, thou sluggard; consider her ways, and be wise," (Prov. 6:6). Or, as Jesus directs, "Consider the lilies of the field, how they grow; they toil not, neither do they spin," (Matt. 6:28). Take the ordinary, or that which may seem ordinary, and make a spiritual application of it to your soul.

The second type of meditation is *solemn meditation,* which is a planned meditation. Here the Christian takes time to consider and contemplate the usefulness of something they have read and studied in the word of God that is familiar to them, in a way that increases their resolution to follow God, or to put off sin, utilizing daily devotions. It may be a thoughtful time on any doctrine or teaching from Scripture that works toward aiding them in their pursuit of holiness.

Meditation is a *duty* as Psalm 1 teaches. It prepares the Christian to see Christ clearly. In this, the minds of believers exercise themselves to such thoughts of the majesty, holiness, and greatness of God, as may prepare them to serve him with reverence and godly fear. Concerning the heralding of the gospel to Mary, "But Mary kept all these things, and pondered them in her heart," (Luke 2:19).

The nature of the duty requires, that this meditation should first respect God himself, *i.e.* what can one find out about God through Christ that needs to be understood more clearly. John Owen said, "God is to be meditated on with respect to his majesty, greatness, and holiness, in all the Christian's addresses to him in all his ordinances. Here the Christian considers his rest in Jesus Christ, his satisfaction and eternal covenant of rest for him through Christ, which are the objects of a suitable meditation."[25] The Christian especially looks to

---

[25] Owen, John, *Hebrews,* Volume 1, (Edinburgh: Banner of Truth Trust, 1998), 746.

the person of the Son of God, whose works and rest are the foundation of their salvation. In Christ they are made partakers of salvation, and this should be well digested in their mind. What does it mean that one is converted by Jesus? What does it mean that one believes on Jesus? What does it mean personally that one is justified, or sanctified, and the like? In such thoughts the Christian should have a continual apprehension of these things, yet, there is always need to call these things over and over to excite them to duty. It is a *stirring* of the soul.[26]

There is no godly blessed believer who can enter into the state of conversion that can think this duty is somehow insignificant to the Christian. The Christian first hears the sacred truth of God's word and then is convinced that it is true. Second, he considers and meditates on it, and sees how much this true word concerns himself. Third, he is in this way affected with these truths, and being so affected by them, it raises holy resolutions towards a more perfect obedience to God's will. Meditation works into his soul those duties and ideas that God loves.[27]

The Christian does not do this duty in a slight manner. For the Christian to delight in meditation, carefully think and ponder something in the act, to pour himself into it, they must set their hearts to meditate on heavenly things. These are *not trivialities*. They concern

---

[26] "... to stir you up by putting you in remembrance," (2 Peter 1:13).
[27] "Consider, not to meditate is the brand of a reprobate." Fenner, William, *29 Sermons on Several Texts of Scripture*, (London: E.T. for John Stafford, 1657) 24.

God and the truth that surround eternity.[28] They concern the fall, sin, salvation through Jesus Christ, and myriads of other important eternal truths. This is an enabling virtue which strengthens the Christian against the assaults of Satan and all the attractions of being earthly minded.

Godly meditation is of itself a weighty matter. The Christian cannot afford to do this duty in a trivial way. "Cursed be he that doeth the work of the LORD deceitfully," (Jer. 48:10). If the Christian is not serious in his duty before God in this, how can he expect to reap any good from it?

The necessity of meditation is set in the idea that those who do it are blessed. It is not enough for a Christian to carry a Bible tucked under their arm. They must meditate on it. They must meditate on it because God gave us his word not simply to know what his word says, and yet many Christians are deficient in this, but also to meditate on the word that it would dwell in the heart. Thomas Watson uses a familiar illustration.[29] Why does a doctor give a prescription to a patient? Why, so the patient can simply read the prescription and know the remedy—or, that he should apply it? He

---

[28] "For thus saith the high and lofty One that inhabiteth eternity, whose name is Holy; I dwell in the high and holy place, with him also that is of a contrite and humble spirit, to revive the spirit of the humble, and to revive the heart of the contrite ones," (Isa. 57:15).

[29] See his work, Watson, Thomas, *The Saint's Spiritual Delight, and a Christian on the Mount, or the Withdrawing Room of Meditation*, (Coconut Creek: Puritan Publications, 2013).

says, "Christians are to use gospel remedies in applying Scripture to them by fruitful meditation."

Without meditation on Scripture, the blessed man will never be godly, and if not godly, he is not blessed and therefore does not really know the way to true happiness. Christians who do not meditate on the word are like pilots without planes, or farmers without farms. How will the simple and plain manner of Scripture, much less its intricate nature, remain in the mind and heart of the Christian without thinking about it in godly meditation. Such truths found in Scripture will never really affect the Christian. In a certain sense, *meditation makes a Christian.*

Consider the actual necessity of meditating in three ways. 1) It is commanded by God. God thinks meditation is important. The blessed man meditates on the word day and night. 2) It pulls the Christian away from the world to high thoughts of God. He does not walk, stand or sit with evil and the wicked. 3) Meditation fuels the Christian's devotional time so they know what to pray, how to pray, what to study, important truth in their study, applying that study to their heart. Like waters that nourish the tree.

Consider some basic rules for daily meditation. Meditation, as with any other spiritual discipline, is first and foremost to glorify of the most high God. "Therefore, whether you eat or drink, or whatever you do, do all to the glory of God," (1 Cor. 10:31). A successful time of meditation catches God's eye. He, in turn, will spiritually bless the one meditating on his word.

Second, consider the chief end of man is divided not only into glorifying God, but also, enjoying him forever. Meditation looks for the blessed path of the righteous, eternal happiness, true happiness in enjoying God. Without meditation, there is no practical knowledge of the way to true happiness.[30]

Third, meditation is a means of grace which spiritually attains both glorifying God, and enjoying him. William Spurstowe said, "The bee does not derive any sweetness to the flower, but by its work it sucks the honey from it. So meditation conveys nothing of worth to the promise of the word, but it draws forth the sweetness and discovers its beauty, because without it, it would never be tasted or discerned."[31] Like the cow, meditation is chewing the cud, over and over and over in the mind.

Fourth, Christians should be mindful of pressing occasional meditation, and that will in turn give them a habit of how to prolong it in solemn meditation. The more one considers the lilies of the field, the more one will meditate in the night watches.

---

[30] "No more can any child of God receive support and consolation from the promises in the hour of temptation, unless he seriously and solemnly ponders and meditates on them." Calamy, Edmund, *The Godly Man's Ark*, Republished by Puritan Publications in 2012, (Originally printed in London: Printed for John Hancock, 1658) 112.
[31] Section 3, Rule 4: Meditate seriously, frequently on the promises, in Spurstowe's *The Wells of Salvation Opened*, (Coconut Creek: Puritan Publications, 2012).

There is a great profit in godly meditation, a wonderful sweetness in it. "May my meditation be sweet to Him; I will be glad in the LORD," (Psalm 104:34). The meditation of a Christian should be sweet to him, and should make him glad in the Lord. Christians must taste the sweetness of Christ in the word, "You have taught me how sweet your words are to my taste," (Psalm 119:102-103). It is one thing to read a promise, and another to *taste* it. Christians are tasters, not merely those who know things. And, it is not enough in this holy duty to do it, but to love it. To meditate on the word of God is part of the essential character, vital duty and persistent practice of every one that is truly blessed. Meditation is the road to true happiness in Christ.

If one is to profit in this, they must find the marrow and sweetness of God and of Christ. Song of Songs 5:16, "His mouth is most sweet, Yes, he is altogether lovely." In and of himself, Jesus Christ is sweet. He is in the meditative mind of the Christian, beheld as gloriously sweet. Without having a sweet delight in the daily meditation, Christians would weary themselves, and they would weary God too. Isaiah 7:13 says, "Will you weary my God also?" Christians should have times of sweet meditation in God and Christ, which in turn would make him delight in them. But when Christians dispel delight, and instead say, "what a weariness is it to serve the Lord," (Malachi 1:13), God becomes as weary as they are. As a matter of fact, such luke-warm service to him is deplorable. God becomes sick of such services. "So then, because you are lukewarm, and neither cold nor hot, I will vomit you out of My mouth," (Rev. 3:16).[32] When duties like godly meditation (which should be the Christians fuel for devotions,) are a burden, they are also a burden to God. When a man is weary of a burden, he will cast it off. Many Christians give up meditating before ever giving a real attempt at hearty, zealous meditations to God. That's because meditating is *work*. The fall of Adam renders all beneficial work difficult. It is far easier to hold onto *feeling something*, than *thinking something*. Instead, Christians ought to work to improve thoughts so feelings will be rightly informed; that such thoughts would quicken their delight in God's service.

Meditation is an act of the heart as much as it is of the head. It is of things divine, but a practical knowledge of them. Mary "pondered all these sayings in her heart," she did not only think of them with her head, but she pondered on them with her heart. Deut. 4:39 says, "Know therefore this day, and consider it in your heart." Meditation is when a man meditates of Christ as to increase his enflamed heart with the love of Christ. It is like a fire that is fanned in order that the fire burns hotter. He meditates of the truths of God to be transformed into them and conformed into the image of

---

[32] "*Lukewarm:* Rev. 3:16, that is, neither hot nor cold, *indifferent*. Such as they who did halt between two thoughts, or opinions, (1 Kings 18:21)." Wilson, Thomas, *A Complete Christian Dictionary*, (London: E. Cotes and are to be sold by Thomas Williams, 1661) 391-392.

Christ. He meditates on sin, not in an ungodly way, but to anatomize it in order to get his heart to hate sin. When the Christian's *heart* is affected with the meditation they are engaged in with the use of their *head*, meditation shall be sweet because it leads somewhere – to being blessed, and to happiness. David says in Psalm 104:34, "My meditation of him shall be sweet." Christians ought to constantly taste the sweetness of God in their thoughts.[33]

Godly meditation makes a difference between you and wicked men. Wicked people never engage in godly meditation. If your question to a person is, "do you meditate on the word of God each day." And they answer, "huh?" You have your answer. To be a godly man or women, part of godliness lies in divine meditation. You are required to hear the truths of God. You must be convinced that they are the truth. You must consider and meditate on them, and investigate how much they concern you personally. Much is lost on the people of God because of lack of reflection. If you do not think about what the word of God says, and you do not consider its words and its teachings, it will do you little good in the end.

---

[33] "Thinking on God is sweet, it ushers in a secret delight into the soul, (Psalm 104:34). My meditation of him shall be sweet. He whose head is got above the clouds, his thoughts are sled aloft, and he hath God in his eye, is full of divine raptures, and cries out as Peter in the transfiguration, Lord, it is good to be here." Watson, Thomas, *Religion Our True Interest*, (London: J. Astwood for Tho. Parkhurst, 1682) 120.

You are to be affected with the truth of the word. What is the purpose of hearing the word or reading the word without being *changed* by it? Being in this way affected by it you will in turn raise holy resolutions towards a more hearty obedience before Christ.[34] Jonathan Edwards, in his *resolutions*, said, "Resolved, to strive to my utmost every week to be brought higher in religion, and to a higher exercise of grace, than I was the week before."[35] He strove to be affected by a higher exercise of grace every week.

Like bible reading, and bible study there is a great and urgent necessity for your daily solemn meditation. These spiritual disciplines are a Christian's daily way of exercising himself in godliness and walking with God. It's how you walk with God *all the day long*. The Scriptures speak about walking with God daily, and constantly. This walking is a picture of persistent communion. It is in contrast with the wicked. Wicked people do not take time to meditate on the word daily. Hear this now, *the wicked do not meditate on the word of God*. In not doing this, they actively scorn it. They are, in fact, practical atheists in this way, even if they do not label themselves as atheists, and they show forth in doing this the mark of reprobation. God tells them to do something, they don't do it, they act as though God

---

[34] "But be ye doers of the word, and not hearers only, deceiving your own selves," (James 1:22).
[35] https://www.apuritansmind.com/the-christian-walk/jonathan-edwards-resolutions/

doesn't exist or his directives don't matter. *Do you do this?*

You may think to yourself, "I've not really ever been taught, or ever heard of a preacher explaining this "duty" to me in my church." That may very well be true. And consider, on this one duty alone we could spend considerable time, many books, sermons and teachings on all its varied facets. Yet, in this one chapter, as it relates to devotions, God has set down in Psalm 1 the difference between the godly and the wicked. And you've *never* heard a preacher preach it? But you might ask yourself, then, "if this is such a necessary duty, why is it that it is so neglected by so many Christians for so many years?" Since its commanded by God, we aren't going to use the excuse that others don't do it so we are not going to. Philippians 4:8 says, "Finally, brethren, whatsoever things are true, whatsoever things are honest, whatsoever things are just, whatsoever things are pure, whatsoever things are lovely, whatsoever things are of good report; if there be any virtue, and if there be any praise, think on these things." *Think.* Think on these things. Continue to think. Don't stop thinking about them. Meditate on them.

"But I don't see the value in doing this, and it simply adds more time to my personal devotions." Lost men do not see the value in following the Lord Jesus Christ until they are made spiritually alive. In any Christian duty, you may not see its value until you experience its *fruit.* Don't give up on something God specifically commands you to do because you think it is hard, or you were previously unaware of how to do it. Let's consider this awareness.

How can you rightly meditate on the word of God? Here are three things you can do to begin divine meditation. First, you must have something to meditate on. This means that if other aspects of devotions are slim to none (bible reading and study) you will never have any fuel to think about. This could be the reason meditation is a scary prospect for you. By neglecting reading and study, there is nothing to meditate. Bible reading and study give your meditations the fuel on which to meditate. Choose a scripture or passage that seems to be important in your daily reading. Or it may be that you are dealing with a theological topic, something you are learning, take time to consider each angle and aspect of it. It could be that you meditate on that idea or that passage or that text for many days, or even weeks or months until you are satisfied that something good has come out of contemplating it. It has changed you in some way.

Second, consider things in the word of God that you have firsthand experience about to meditate on; doctrines you should be familiar with. Repentance. Sin. Christ's life, work, death, resurrection, heavenly intercession. Temptation. The Trinity. God's eternal covenant. Spiritual Strength. Divine illumination. Heaven and Hell. If you have a hard time considering what might be most important, or those things which concern you specifically, use the *1647 Westminster Confession* and allow the *Larger or Shorter Catechism* to guide you into sections of the Bible that are most important to see the way of happiness clearly.

Third, set aside a specific amount of time, and begin small. No one begins meditating perfectly. There are many excellent works that deal with divine meditation that you can acquire which will lead you through meditation. The puritans wrote forty-five whole treatises on the subject. I've published a few of those and have quite a few more in the lineup on such an important topic. The ones I like best are those that give you actual meditation to read so you can consider how to think about some key biblical topics.[36]

Let me give you a brief example of a meditation of Jesus Christ in his heavenly intercession. Our devotional time is set, let's assume, in the book of Hebrews. We read Hebrews 7:25, "Therefore He is also able to save to the uttermost those who come to God through him, since he always lives to make intercession for them." So, how shall I consider this?

> This seems to be a promise. The idea of "promise" could be a meditation in itself, but we stick to the idea that God has *made us* a promise. This promise is about salvation and the prevailing intercession of Christ, who now sits on the right

---

[36] You can find those by Richard Allestree, Thomas White and John Ball at Puritan Publications.

62

hand of God in glory. When he was on earth, he purchased, by the price of his blood, all the spiritual benefits and riches both of grace and glory that are held within this promise. He gave all these benefits to believers. "Them." I'm a them. I'm a believer. I have come to him. He brought me to himself. Christ is able to save me and I demonstrate what the Psalmist told me in shunning evil and walking in the way of righteousness. He saves me by his life and death and resurrection. But I know there is more. The text tells me there is more. Through the cross I find he attained salvation for me. But though he attains salvation for me, there must be some means by which believers obtain it, and Jesus delivers it. The means of applying all this to me are at his resurrection and intercession. What is the meaning of this resurrection? God's Messiah doesn't stay in the grave. The power of death has no power over him. His resurrection is God's approval of the Messiah's work in his life and on the Cross. God the Father approved of all his work, and his infinite sacrifice and death, and so did not leave him in the tomb. A dead Savior, that is *an oxymoron*. A dead Savior in the tomb is no Savior. This Jesus, though, always lives to make intercession for me if I am a godly blessed man. He is not dead, and if he is the Messiah, God's anointed one, he cannot be dead. His resurrection declares his conquest over death. But you also know, God did not stop there. I always hear preachers telling me about the life, death and resurrection of Christ, but what about his ascension and intercession for me? I know from reading the Gospel in all sorts of places that Jesus says the Father listens to him, and all his requests are answered as the Son in whom he is well pleased. His intercession even shows God's favor and acceptance with the Father. Through Christ, I reach the Father. Jesus is, right now, in heaven, interceding for me. All that he asks of the Father, on my behalf, the Father grants, and I receive. Christ intercedes on behalf of all those for whom he died, and died for all those for whom he would intercede. As a believer, he saves me to the uttermost. And in saving me to the uttermost, he does this in part through interceding for me at present. As a believer I am secured in everything, as an heir, to the spiritual benefits which he has purchased. He is in fact the great High Priest. He is greater than all other priests. He is the highest Priest in heaven. He has ascended into heaven, a sanctuary which no other priest could ever enter into or sit down in — all their sacrifices being imperfect and therefore to be daily renewed by them when they ministered them in the temple. Jesus is the Son of God, and who is the only favorite of the Father in heaven, and he is my Advocate, and continually petitions God to fulfill his covenant made with him. My prayers made to him, are brought to the Father on my behalf. What could possibly hinder or weaken my faith which the intercession of Christ does not fully remove and take away? He gives me all things for life and godliness. He saves me, not sort-of, but to the uttermost. I sin all the time, but I am interceded for by this risen Christ all the time. It is his only work in heaven to intercede for sinners (Hebrews 7:25). He has, in his person, a fullness of all perfections which may assure me and every believer that the promises which he pleads to God will be granted. I must, then, exercise faith in this Savior, who is in heaven right now, pleading his blood for my soul.

Do you see that your heart can be filled with such things with strong consolations, with stirring your soul up, when, by the eye of faith, you look on this one promise, of Christs blood and the matter of his most powerful intercession? But this only occurs when you take the time to meditate on the word. And such meditation is sweet, a delight, and is constant for the blessed man or woman in Christ. Because, godly meditation makes a spiritual difference in God's Kingdom between you and wicked men, for godly meditation is the way, the only way, to a knowledge of rest in true happiness; where wicked men will always reject it.

Mark 3: Daily Prayer

"Behold, he prays," (Acts 9:11).

In Acts 9:1-11 we find Saul, the murderer, converted. "Then Saul, still breathing threats and murder against the disciples of the Lord, went to the high priest and asked letters from him to the synagogues of Damascus, so that if he found any who were of the Way, whether men or women, he might bring them bound to Jerusalem," (Acts 9:1-2). Saul, the murdering, hard-hearted Pharisee, was threatening believers of the Way, and breathing out threats desiring to kill all those who confessed to be part of body of Christ. His name, *Saul*, means *desire*. In this instance, his desire was to uphold his murderous ways. The words of this wicked and depraved diabolical man could not quickly enough come off his tongue, that while breath was still in his mouth murderous thoughts, accusations and plans were being spewed out. Satanic opposition fell from his lips. His sole purpose was to destroy the work of the Gospel. Saul, here, at this stage, was a pawn of the cursed adversary *the devil*. He was looking to destroy any shred of the Gospel on the planet – before it spread. He did not love Jesus Christ all his life. He was a murderous, unconverted wretch for a good portion of his life. He loved his own conception of God, and this Jesus was at odds with *his* religion and *his* kingdom.

Going to the Jewish High Priest, the highest Jewish authority in their midst, Saul sought papers and allowances, for his blatantly homicidal plans to be given a seal of approval. This not only allowed him free reign to kill followers of the Way, but allowed him to have a pass from the highest Jewish authority in the land to protect his own skin lest anyone judge his actions in the Jewish faith, as too harsh. He was threatening murder and slaughter and even seeking admiration for it. He looked for the utter destruction of the Way, the unqualified annihilation of those following the radical rabbi Jesus who had been crucified among thieves as a heretic and purveyor of some new Way, supposedly seen in some *fabled* resurrection. Clever Saul did not give a single moment's thought or credence to the truth of such a wild claim as a physical, manifested resurrection, even being a Pharisee who believed in a resurrection. Saul wanted to murder these deluded daydreamers in a demonic and zealous massacre. He desired to drag them out of their homes, put them in jail, kill them a dozen different ways. He wanted to make sure that there is no root to this newfangled movement that claimed to have a corner on *messianic* fulfillment.

With murderous intentions, on his way to Damascus, Saul's conversion to Jesus Christ was nothing short of miraculous.[1] As one born out of time,

---

[1] A miracle is a visible, wonderful work, done by the Almighty power of God, above, or against the course of nature, to confirm some divine truth. It was limited to three cycles, the cycle of Moses and the Israelites in Egypt, the cycle of Elijah and Elisha, and the

Christ himself, the Son of Man appears to him on the road. The text says, "As he journeyed he came near Damascus, and suddenly a light shone around him from heaven. Then he fell to the ground, and heard a voice saying to him, "Saul, Saul, why are you persecuting Me?" Consider, a glimpse of Christ's glory was given to the church in his transfiguration in Matt. 17:2, "And he was transfigured before them, and his face did shine as the sun, and his raiment was white as the light." When he appeared to Saul from heaven, his body was wonderfully glorious in its risen and ascended exalted state. The curtains of heaven rolled back, as it were like a scroll, and he appeared in incomprehensible majestic light to *Saul.* Saul *could not endure* the light which shined to him from heaven round about. He was cast to the ground, he *fell,* the word meaning actually, *prostrated* on the ground, and Christ asked him why he was running after God's people in defiant hostility. Saul asks, "Who are You, Lord?" Saul has it correct: *Lord.* "Then the Lord said, "I am Jesus, whom you are persecuting. It is hard for you to kick against the goads." This is as if Christ said, "Do you not see Saul that it is hard for you to rebel against me? I am the sovereign one; who are you little man to think you can do anything against or over my will?" Consider Saul's constant, thorough, attempt at rebelling against Christ. To rebel against the body of

cycle of Jesus and the Apostles. See Gouge, William, *A Learned and Very Useful Commentary on the Whole Epistle to the Hebrews,* London: A.M., T.W. and S.G. for Joshua Kirton, 1655) 130-150.

Christ is to rebel against *Christ.* Christ spoke to him in his native tongue, in Hebrew, as Acts 26 give's Paul's account of his conversion. "So he, trembling and astonished, said, "Lord, what do You want me to do?" Then the Lord said to him, "Arise and go into the city, and you will be told what you must do." Here is found an immediate change, an immediate professing submission. Take note, Christ *always* welcomes penitent sinners. Fearful and horrified, Saul inquires what he must do out of necessity, and the Lord tells him that he is to go into the city, and he will be instructed at the proper time, in Christ's good time, what he must do.

Saul was changed, converted. How do we know? Paul's testimony adds much to this, when he says later, "But rise and stand on your feet; for I have appeared to you for this purpose, to make you a minister and a witness both of the things which you have seen and of the things which I will yet reveal to you," (Acts 26:16). *Christ* changes Saul and converts him to be a light to the Gentiles. Christ will use this murderous wretch, and change him into a Gospel light.

The text further says, "And the men who journeyed with him stood speechless, hearing a voice but seeing no one." Christ appeared for the expressed purpose of converting this homicidal rascal, appearing only to him, though others heard the voice. "Then Saul arose from the ground, and when his eyes were opened he saw no one. But they led him by the hand and brought him into Damascus. And he was three days without sight, and neither ate nor drank," (Acts 9:3-9). He saw before, but was blind. He is blinded now, but he sees. He sees being born again, but he is physically blinded.

"Now there was a certain disciple at Damascus named Ananias; and to him the Lord said in a vision, "Ananias." And he said, "Here I am, Lord." So the Lord said to him, "Arise and go to the street called Straight, and inquire at the house of Judas for one called Saul of Tarsus, for behold, he prays," (Acts 9:10-11). Christ visits Ananias in a vision, and he is instructed to go to Saul of Tarsus. "Behold, he prays." An astounding commentary by Jesus Christ to Ananias, that in the act of demonstrating his Spirit's power over the murderous wretch, and converting him for his appointment, Christ points out, "behold," *take note*, "he prays." Right humiliation demonstrates the work of radical reformation of heart. That's true godly-sorrow indeed that works repentance *not to be repented of,* (2 Cor. 7:10).

No sooner was this murdering wretch, "Saul of Tarsus" converted, then it was said of him, by God, "Behold, he prays," (Acts 9:11). It is no wonder that almost all his letters to the churches begin and end with prayer. This is a *distinguishing* means to promote genuine devotion to God; and the regular and conscientious practice of this duty is one of the best evidences of the sincere and converted Christian. This will be the doctrine to consider from this text, for the chapter at hand.

DOCTRINE: one of the best signs of the converted Christian is participating in daily, persistent prayer. True repentance before Christ in conversion always has a garnish – prayer. As if the converted sinner thinks to himself, "Well I must have grace, and I will never give up, until I have grace. I will never leave seeking and waiting, and striving with God, and my own heart, until he draws me by the power of his grace afresh each day I seek it." When Paul was breathing out persecution against the saints, God soon reformed his course—and situated him in prayer. "Behold, he prays." This was the evidence to Ananias.[2]

Those who are in a state of grace, who have been changed and given the Spirit, have the Spirit of prayer. The apostle Paul, as soon as he is translated from darkness by Christ, into the kingdom of light, of Christ, the kingdom of the Father's beloved Son, now has this sincere character trait, "Behold, he prays," (Acts 9:11). Christ's commentary on the converted man is the submission of his will in prayer. Had he prayed before? Yes, he prayed as a Pharisee, as a hypocrite. Now, however, he prayed working from Christ's merit and account, Christ's Spirit, rather than only in his own

---

[2] A converted man "must (in respect of the frequent intercourse of his heart with God, in frequent ejaculations and breathings of soul) be as a man wholly resolved into that duty [of prayer], as Paul was at his first conversion, who (as that expression (behold he prays) doth intimate) seems to have been *all prayer*, and wholly taken up with that duty." Gilpin, Richard, *Demonologia sacra, or, A Treatise of Satan's Temptations in Three Parts*, (London: J.D. for Richard Randal and Peter Maplasden, 1677), 214.

strength. Now, he prayed in the Holy Spirit, as Jude says.[3] The Spirit of grace and supplication is peculiar to the saints in this way. Out of the gate, "behold, he prays."

Consider also, for a moment, that he neither ate nor drank anything for three days while in prayer before Ananias arrives. Two spiritual disciplines are immediately employed, fasting *and* prayer. The text says he fasted; a *note* made by the Holy Spirit. Here is seen his utter self-denial. The opposite of his course not long ago was selfish ambition. Yet, the immediacy of Christ's comment on his conversion is ... he is a great theologian isn't he Ananias. No, that is not what the Lord says. Does he say he is a great teacher? No. Christ says, "behold, he prays."

A demonstration of conversion is a constant, daily devotional prayer time. When Christians come to pray many times before God, it is a sincere sign that they seek God himself, when no one but God knows they are seeking him. Prayer aids the Christian to thrive in grace in this way. Upon his conversion Saul immerses himself in three days of fasting and prayer while *blind.* Some may have rushed off to the doctor. Some may have called a friend or neighbor to help. This converted man utterly submits himself and calls to God for direction. His heart was overwhelmed with need and petitioned the throne of Christ in prayer. God's testimony of him is that he prays.

---

[3] "But ye, beloved, building up yourselves on your most holy faith, praying in the Holy Ghost," (Jude 1:20).

What is prayer? Prayer is basic to the Christian. Prayer is a duty commanded all through Scripture which is part of private devotions, one of three legs to the spiritual chair. As covered in the previous two chapters, devotion to God is made up of bible reading and study, godly meditation and now is added *prayer.* God has ordained these as a means of grace specifically for the good of the Christian. Believers should take this to heart.

Christians are to be *persistent* in prayer like Jacob, (Gen. 32:24–30), Moses, (Exod. 33:12–16; 34:9), Elijah, (1 Kings 18:24–44), the two blind men of Jericho, (Matt. 20:30-31; Mark 10:48; Luke 18:39), the Syrophoenician woman, (Matt. 15:22–28; Mark 7:25–30), and the centurion, (Matt. 8:5; Luke 7:3-4). All who prayed, did so *fervently* to God. Christians are commanded to be generally prayerful, "My voice You shall hear in the morning, O LORD; In the morning I will direct it to You, And I will look up," (Psa. 5:3). "Now when Daniel knew that the writing was signed, he went home. And in his upper room, with his windows open toward Jerusalem, he knelt down on his knees three times that day, and prayed and gave thanks before his God, as was his custom since early days," (Dan. 6:10). "For God is my witness, whom I serve with my spirit in the gospel of his Son, that without ceasing I make mention of you always in my prayers," (Rom. 1:9).[4] They have an engaged mind to God and yearning heart.

Jesus' example of personal prayer was constant, solitary, sometimes took place up a mountain, and in varied circumstances. "And when he had sent the multitudes away, he went up on the mountain by himself to pray. Now when evening came, he was alone there," (Matt. 14:23).[5] It was in various places such as Gethsemane, (Matt. 26:36; Mark 14:32; Luke 22:45), before the day begins, (Mark 1:35), while he was in distress, (John 12:27; Heb. 5:7), in the wilderness, (Luke 5:16), and on behalf of other people (Luke 22:31-32; John 17).

The Children's Shorter Catechism in Question 105 asks, "What is prayer?" The answer is given, "Prayer is asking God for things which he has promised to give." How does one know what he promises to give? It's in his word. Jesus places all these spiritual disciplines together when he says, "If you abide in Me, and *My words* abide in you, you will ask what you desire, and it shall be done for you," (John 15:7). Prayer and the word are intrinsically linked. That is because the Christian's desires are God's desires because they know his will, because they know his word. Those promises are found *in his word.* "Now this is the confidence that we have in him, that if we ask anything *according to his will*, he

---

[4] See Psalm 5:1-3; 42:8; 109:4; 116:2; Dan. 6:10; Luke 2:37; Acts 6:4; Acts 10:2, 9; Rom. 1:9; Rom. 12:12; Eph. 1:15-16; Col. 1:9; 1 Thess. 3:10; 1 Thess. 5:17; 1 Tim. 5:5; 2 Tim. 1:3.

[5] Matt. 14:23; Mark 6:46; Luke 6:12; 9:28.

hears us. And if we know that he hears us, whatever we ask, we know that we have the petitions that we have asked of Him," (1 John 5:14-15). Prayer is not done "willy nilly." Prayer is based on Scripture. Prayer is the language of Scripture. Without knowing Scripture, it is very difficult for God to say of that one, "Behold, he prays." Instead, God would say, behold, he talks. Behold, he babbles. Behold, he surely isn't *praying*, for praying takes the word of God and sends the word back to heaven in pleas and requests.

Consider some definitions of prayer. There are theological definitions and practical definitions. Practical definitions are heart-felt. Theological definitions give the Christian the concept itself. Thomas Gouge defines prayer as "a right opening of the desire of the heart to God in the name of Jesus Christ."[6] *The 1647 Westminster Shorter Catechism* question 98 defines it as "an offering up of our desires to God, for things agreeable to his will, in the name of Christ, with confession of our sins, and thankful acknowledgment of his mercies." Thomas Watson said prayer, "is the soul breathing itself into the bosom of its heavenly Father."[7] A prayer to "God, through Christ, with faith, is that which I ask for graces wanting, and give thanks for

[6] Gouge, Thomas, *The Works of Thomas Gouge*, (London: E and E Hosford Printers, 1815) 475.
[7] Watson, Thomas, *The Lord's Prayer*, (electronic version, 2005) Section (3) [1].

benefits received."[8] Those definitions are very *heart-felt* practical definitions.

As much as practical definitions abound, practical definitions must also be tied to understanding the *essence* of prayer. Prayer is the Scriptures (the will of God) formed into an argument and retorted back to God again to remind him what he has said in his word. Prayer is not something that moves God, but simply reminds him of his will already promised to the believer. People hear TV Evangelists telling people to "claim the promises" as if its magic. No, no, in the right manner, *claim the promises*. Remind God what he has already said. Stand on his will, know his will so it may be prayed. "Thy *will* be done on earth as it is in heaven." Prayer, then, would be leaning on the promises already stated in the Bible, but given back to God for the Christian's own benefit. "O Lord you say that..." and then the prayer is given according to the word. And if it is according to the word, it is according to God's will. Prayer is a confession of sin within the language of guilt, but it is also the articulation of worship of an intelligent soul. It is all of this bound up together. It is the mind informing the tongue expressing the yearning of the heart according to Scripture. Prayer is the expression of what Christians know to be true about God and his will based on what they know the word of God says. It is, then impossible to pray without knowing Scripture. The less one knows

---

[8] Horne, Robert, *Points of Instruction for the Ignorant*, (London: George Purslowe for Francis Burton, 1617) electronic version.

of the bible, the less one is equipped to pray well. It is a lifting up of the mind, and a pouring out of the heart before God.[9]

When Christians pray, whether it is a retorting of God's word back to him or a breathing of the soul into him, it should always be done according to God's will. "Teach me to do thy will," (Psa. 143:10). "I delight to do thy will," (Psa. 40:8). "Thy will be done, as in heaven, so in earth," (Luke 11:2). Why is this? Prayer is not primarily beneficial for God but beneficial for the believer. Is prayer going to change the mind of God? No, not at all. The Christian's prayers are to *align to God's will*. This is the essence of submission.[10] God is immutable; that means he does not change. "For I the LORD do not change," (Mal. 3:6). But his will is always accomplished.

God's will is executed many times by secondary causes. Secondary causes are those tools God uses outside of himself to affect a particular decree. Want to know that God's decrees are working in the midst of a believer's life – "behold, *he prays.*" He prays according to God's will and that prayer is the means by which God's decrees effect change in the circumstance. One might ask, "A believer's prayer makes up the means of a decree?" Yes, most assuredly and quite often. God uses prayers as the means to compliment his decrees. "Elijah

---

[9] Greenham, Richard, *The Works of the Reverend and Faithfull Servant of Jesus Christ Mr. Richard Greenham*, (London: Thomas Snodham and Thomas Creede for William Welby, 1612) 90.
[10] "Submit yourselves therefore to God," (James. 4:7).

was a man with a nature like ours, and he prayed earnestly that it would not rain; and it did not rain on the land for three years and six months. And he prayed again, and the heaven gave rain, and the earth produced its fruit," (James 5:17-18). Mountains can be moved by the effectual fervent prayer of the righteous man, for it avails much. Why? Because he prays God's will, taken from Scripture. Prayer, then, is the believer's mind conforming to God's will and reminding God what he said in his word for the Christian's good.

There are seven basic parts to prayer. First, there is adoration. Adoring God is the primary business of believer. Adoration is vitally linked to the view of God's majesty and being. It adores God because of who he is, rather than simply what he has done. It's often the case that Christians spend much time thanking God for what he has done for them and in them, rather than spending time adoring the excellence of his being. It is hard to adore God for who he is for that rests on knowing God's attributes. Knowing God is both about who he is first, and then what he does second. Though this is an essential part of prayer, it is the most neglected since adoring God in this fashion would require a level of knowledge of who he is instead of simply what he has done for them. It involves the intricacies of theology, especially the doctrine of God.[11] Knowing more about God allows the believer to adore him more. "Give unto

---

[11] See my work on the doctrine of God, *Sparks of Divine Glory, A Practical Study of the Attributes of God*, in two volumes.

the LORD the glory due to his name; Worship the LORD in the beauty of holiness," (Psa. 29:2). But what if one does not really understand *holiness?* What if he does not really *know God's name?*

Second, the next aspect of prayer is *praise*. This is a kind of adoration, but it is viewed in the context of his will. It is the apprehension of the outworking of his decrees and desires upon the earth. God is praised for his works in all he does.[12] He has the power to accomplish great and mighty things "that you know not," (Jer. 33:3). He is able to accomplish them and bring his holy will to pass in every circumstance according to his pure, righteous and holy desire. This, though, is contained in the substance of Christ's directive "thy will be done." Aligning one's self with God's will is where prayer is effective. When a Christian sees such a display of God's power (even in the varied acts of creation) he bursts forth into praise to the work of the Almighty. "Prayer also will be made for Him continually, and daily he shall be praised." (Psa. 72:15). In private devotions Christians should have a time of praise and consider, "What can I praise you for today?"

Third, a most common aspect of prayer is confession. It is a declaration by the Christian to God in regard to sin. It is the language of repentance and guilt. It comes forth from a heart that knows it is sinful and imperfect. It is filled with humility and submission. Here

---

[12] "Bless the LORD, all his works in all places of his dominion: bless the LORD, O my soul," (Psa. 103:22).

the Christian pours forth the transgressions, both secret and presumptuous, before the open face of God. "I acknowledged my sin to You, and my iniquity I have not hidden. I said, "I will confess my transgressions to the LORD," And You forgave the iniquity of my sin," (Psa. 32:5). He confesses that he has not done what God says, and that he does things that God forbids. He seeks forgiveness for both through Jesus Christ.[13]

Fourth, is supplication, the actual entreaty for the forgiveness and pardon for the confessed sin. It is one thing to confess, but quite another to ask forgiveness for the sin committed. Confession is not supplication. They are vitally interrelated but they are still set on their own. It would be a neglect of prayer to simply, and generally, ask for forgiveness of sin and never become specific with those transgressions which have been committed. It would be like saying, "Lord, please forgive me for all of my sins..." *God knows* the sins of the believer. He desires *the believer* to be intimately aware of how they sinned against him and change as a result. It is equally true to neglect entreating God for real forgiveness if one simply confessed sin in general. So, these are not mutually exclusive in practice, though they are in defining them. They will be very specific about their sin, "Deliver me from the guilt of bloodshed," (Psa. 51:14).

Fifth, there is petition. This implies a sense of need awakened by the soul. It is the sense of the soul

---

[13] "In whom we have redemption through his blood, even the forgiveness of sins," (Col. 1:14).

which experiences the need (whatsoever that may be). It is the need existing and felt and delivered to the throne room of Christ. Petitions may be about anything, to a degree. Christians are not to petition the throne for things they simply want, as if asking for $1,000,000 each day, or a new pool would be spiritually beneficial or suitable for prayer. Christians are going to think *biblically* about petitions. When they petition God, there is a need, a need which exists in the life of the Christian as something affecting his walk and life that needs fixing or spiritual vigor. It is not simply a worldly desire, although in certain cases a temporary need may be a desire to fulfill the spiritual connectiveness the Christian has with God; such might be entirely acceptable. The Christian may have a felt need to apply for a new job and needs guidance as to where God may desire him. It is something which he is experiencing in his whole being, and it is something which is a necessary need in his life to be answered either for the growth of grace in his soul, or the need of that which may be daily – like daily bread in all its forms. The answers may differ but the legitimacy of the petition is something to be prayed every day. "Deliver me, O LORD, from my enemies," (Psa. 143:9). "And do not lead us into temptation, but deliver us from the evil one," (Matt. 6:13). Whether delivered from enemies or delivered from sin, both are spiritually related to the supplication the Christian entreats Christ to answer.

Sixthly, thanksgiving, or gratitude for the relief given of the need, is another aspect of the Christian's prayer life which is essential. When relief is given to a particular need (let's say a man finds that job they have been hunting for over the last two months comes through) then thanksgiving resounds. Sometimes answers for particular requests come, but they are not really the answers believers are looking for. "Now when they had gone through Phrygia and the region of Galatia, they were forbidden by the Holy Spirit to preach the word in Asia. After they had come to Mysia, they tried to go into Bithynia, but the Spirit did not permit them. So passing by Mysia, they came down to Troas. And a vision appeared to Paul in the night. A man of Macedonia stood and pleaded with him, saying, "Come over to Macedonia and help us," (Acts 16:6-9). What an odd answer. There were people needing the Gospel, but the Holy Spirit forbid Paul from going. Nevertheless, there is still an element of relief which accompanies an answered prayer, even if the answer is "no" or "wait" or "go somewhere else." In these cases thanksgiving may be more difficult, but it is never excused. As God guides the Christian, the Christian remains thankfully submissive.

Lastly, prayer should have a focused expression of intercession. Intercession is a possession of a common understanding to pray for another's needs. It means believers are not selfish with their prayer time and the "our Father" who art in heaven, really weighs heavily on their heart to pray for others. *Our Father*, not simply *my*

Father. The burdens of other church members and believers in their association with church members, should be something which lays heavy on their heart. They take these burdens, these requests, and petitions to the throne room of Christ in the stead of others. The multiplicity of prayer warriors lifting up needs for the soul of a downcast brother is proportionally more "effective" and elicits a desire from the whole church (a local church or churches) to share in the desires for relief for their brothers or sisters. The Bible is filled with exhortations to pray for one another. For example, "For this reason we also, since the day we heard it, do not cease to pray for you, and to ask that you may be filled with the knowledge of his will in all wisdom and spiritual understanding," (Col. 1:9).

Consider a side note on the attitude of the believer in prayer as stated in 1 Thess. 5:17. 1 Thessalonians 5:17 teaches the frame and disposition of the Christian's attitude toward prayer. "Pray without ceasing." "Behold, he prays..." how? "...without ceasing." There, Ananias, you will find him praying, continually. His whole life is built on it.

Believers should be in a constant frame of prayer, ready to lift up their voice in supplication, adoration and thanksgiving to the Almighty God in every providence, whether it is frowning or otherwise. 1 Thessalonians 5:17 teaches the frame of heart and attitude towards prayer; that its frame is ready to pray always. Pray, as outlined before, yet, now, *without ceasing.* "But I give myself to prayer," (Psa. 109:4). This refers to the believer's attitude in the act of prayer. It is true, he cannot *pray always*. He must eat. He must attend his work. He must attend worship and hear sermons. He must spend time with his children, and such. He must sleep. The verse does not mean continue to pray in an act that never ends, physically speaking. It *does mean* that the attitude of the Christian is one which sets his face toward praying always. He is ready to pray always. He is in a constant attitude of praying. Nathaniel Vincent who wrote the best extra biblical work on prayer says, "God's word of command should cause us perpetually to stand in awe. We must not dare to cease doing that which he would have us employed in without ceasing."[14] He continues, "To pray always implies praying in every state and condition; in sickness, in health, in prosperity, in adversity, prayer is to be used; without prayer, sickness will be unsanctified, and an uncomfortable load; and if it is taken off, it will be in anger; without prayer, health will be a judgment, and only serve to encourage a neglect of the soul and another world. Without prayer, adversity will be intolerable, and prosperity will be a snare, an occasion of forgetfulness of God, and a daring to rebel against him. No condition should cause a cessation of prayer; for the apostle says, "pray without ceasing," (1 Thessalonians 5:17)."

---

[14] See Vincent's work in full, *The Spirit of Prayer*, (Coconut Creek: Puritan Publications, 2013).

Prayer shows that you acknowledge God. You might think, "Of course I acknowledge God, I'm a Christian!" Then, "behold, he prays." We acknowledge that Christ is a *real God* when we pray. "But without faith it is impossible to please him, for he who comes to God must believe that he is, and that he is a rewarder of those who diligently seek him," (Heb. 11:6). Behold, he prays. We diligently seek him.

We acknowledge his providence and sovereignty over our lives. *The Lord's Prayer* in Matthew 6 demonstrates time and time again our need of God: our need of his Kingdom, his will, our daily bread, to be delivered from temptation, and such. Prayer often demonstrates that Christians who pray effectively always believe in the sovereignty of God in everything. "O God, I will have a good day today because I will exercise my will effectively without your help." Who would say this? "O God I don't need to ask you to open up anyone's heart to receive the Gospel, for they don't need your help because they can exercise their will to save themselves." No one prays like this. Everyone always prays like a Christian submitted before God's sovereignty. "O Lord help." "O Lord save." In this kind of submission, you are held up in the hand of the Almighty, in the Covenant of Grace, in the Son of his love, transferred from the dominion of darkness to the kingdom of light, and he desires to say of you, "behold, she prays, ... he prays."

Prayer must be more than merely acknowledging God. It must be adoration of him, and a complete surrender in casting all your cares on him for ... he cares for you. Saul casts himself upon the ground, not once, but twice, in homage to the Lord on the road, and worship to the Lord in prayer. Prayer should be your exclamation as a new creature, a holy duty working you into a temper and attitude of humility. Zech. 12:10, "I will pour upon the house of David, and the inhabitants of Jerusalem, the spirit of grace and of supplication." Do you have the Spirit of grace and supplication? Do you have humility? Like Saul, a broken spirit is a humble spirit. "But to this man will I look, even to him that is poor, and of a contrite spirit," (Isa. 66:2). "I dwell in the high and holy place with him also that is of a contrite and humble spirit," (Isa. 57:15). It shows a love to Jesus Christ. A broken praying spirit is a tender affectionate loving spirit, and this love kindles zealously towards Christ. There's much of Christ in the broken heart. How then can a broken heart choose but to be endeared to Christ in prayer? This cultivates obedience—because a spirit like Saul's, who prays, is an obedient dutiful spirit. "And I will give them a heart of flesh—there is the contrite spirit—that they may walk in my statutes and keep my ordinances and do them—there is obedience with a lowly heart, (Ezek. 11:19-20, 36:26-27). St. Augustine said, "Lord, give me ability to do what you command and then command me whatever you please."[15] Do you have such a dutiful spirit as that?

Without a healthy prayer life, without *acknowledging God* in that way, you engage in practical atheism. What does that mean? Atheists don't pray. They might offer a prayer, or try prayer, if they get into a sticky situation, but they place that on the same level as a horoscope or opening a fortune cookie. Christians copy practical atheists when they do not *give* themselves to prayer, or do not pray as God requires them to. Their lives are to be in submission to his will and in submission to it as laid out in Scripture. God becomes angry with his people, and complains of their neglect of him when they do not pray. Jeremiah 2:32, "My people have forgotten me days without number." Do you go many days without number in prayer?[16]

There must be a strategy for personal prayer. Thomas Gouge wisely said, "Do not dare to attempt anything until you have commended yourself, and your affairs to God by prayer in the morning."[17] This is very wise advice. Start your day with God.

---

[15] Augustine's *Confessions*, 10:29.

[16] "As religion is the life of the soul, so prayer is the soul of religion, and the breath by which it lives and moves, without which it is stifled up and dies. It is a piece of service, as most acceptable to God, so most useful to us: for as in it we make our daily acknowledgment, and do homage as it were to the Great King, so in it we have continual access into his high court, to offer up our petitions to him, to make known our wants, and implore his gracious relief." Hammond, Henry, *The Daily Practice of Devotion,* (London: Printed for R. Royston, 1684) 1-2.

[17] Gouge, *Works*, 127ff.

Consider that God will reward you in your diligent praying. Christ said, "Thy Father which seeth in secret shall reward thee openly," (Matthew 6:6). Have a *solid* commitment for personal prayer. This should press you to have a *strategy* in prayer. It is giving God the first fruits of the day, and the last fruits at its end.

Keeping it introductory and simple, prayer is to the Father, through Christ, in the power of the Spirit – it is reminding God of his promises. This means that you have to know the word to pray effectively. It's more than simply asking God to bless our day, or bless this or that. Effective prayer is prayer aligned with God's will as discerned from scripture. If you are unware of the content of Scripture it will almost be impossible to pray well. The thief on the cross sent up a prayer to Christ of sorts, even in the midst of his last moments on earth. "Remember me when you come into your kingdom," (Luke 23:42). There is quite a bit in that statement, a kind of prayer. The Lordship of Christ. The submission to beseech or pray to him in petition. The awareness of the kingdom of God. Submission before the sovereignty of God. The personal and intimate address of one who could come to the place where grace would be found boldly. Hope in Christ. Faith in Christ, *etc.* Know the promises in Scripture, so you can pray them to him. Remind God what he has said to you in the word. Claim the promises in that way.[18] It does not have to be a

---

[18] "We must claim the promises, whence comes the stability of God's children. ... This should direct us in our dealing with God, not

constant repetition of "God you said...so..." Rather, it is the general principle you glean from passages you know apply to a given situation, which can be further applied to your petitions that argue their purpose so that God listens to his word. Such as, "Lord, the Bible says that you are the one who changes hearts, and converts souls. My friend needs to be converted. I ask that you would convert him."

In the morning, let God come in first to your heart before everyone and everything else. The devil will attempt to fill it with worldly cares and desires, so that it will grow unfit for the service of God for the rest of the day. Now, consider, not giving God your dopey time, but at the same time, giving him the first fruits. Thomas Gouge said, "If your business is urgent and great, rise sooner; do not dare to attempt anything, until you have commended yourself, and your affairs to God by prayer. If you take any little liberty to omit this duty, the Devil will so work on you, that little by little you will become weary of it, if God's grace is not more powerful in you."[19] He will wear you down until you begin to chip away at doing what would be spiritual beneficial.

---

to go directly to him, but by a promise. And when we have a promise, look to Christ, in whom it is performed. If we ask anything of God in Christ's name, he will give it us, John 14:13. If we thank God for anything, thank him in Christ, that we have it in him. What a comfort is this, that we may go to God in Christ and claim the promises boldly, because he loves us with the same love he bears to his only beloved Son." Sibbes, Richard, *The Complete Works of Richard Sibbes,* Volume 4, (Edinburgh: Banner of Truth Trust, 1982) 120.

[19] Ibid.

Begin every day with God's word and prayer. Lewis Bayly said to start your morning prayer like this, "My soul waits on you, O Lord, more than the morning watch watches for the morning! O God, therefore be merciful to me, and bless me, and cause your face to shine on me! Fill me with your mercy this morning, so shall I rejoice and be glad all my days."[20] All of this is the language of the psalmist. *Wake up with God.* Should he not be addressed by you first upon your rising? Reminding you that he has given you another day in his service which you acknowledge?[21]

Your prayers will always be cold and or shallow unless they are fueled by the word. It is no wonder why so many have a difficult time in personal prayer because they do not know, not only how to pray, but what the language of prayer should sound like because they are unfamiliar with the word. Did you know that prayer has a specific language? Look to the psalms, they are prayers and contemplations put to music, put to poetry, with a constant theme specific to the language of prayer. If you don't read, study and meditate on the word, prayer will be hard for you. It will be a drudgery after a time because it will become the same things said over and over and over. You get stuck in praying with specific words and

---

[20] See Bayly's work, *The Practice of Piety*, in full.
[21] You should also keep in mind that God ought never to receive your dopey time. If you are not awake, or sleepy, or tired, give him a time that best suits him and that you can pray well. Or, find a way to utilize the morning, by planning ahead in some way. Maybe you need to wake up a bit earlier to set the morning aright?

specific phrases over and over, and you do it because you have not expanded your vocabulary of prayer. It is not expanded because you have not expanded your vocabulary of theological and practical ideas about who God is and what he does. They in turn become those cold prayers that freeze before reaching heaven. Much less, Christ forbids such kinds of praying with repetition of the same thing over and over. He says, "And when you pray, do not use vain repetitions as the heathen do. For they think that they will be heard for their many words," (Matt. 6:7). Vain repetition is monotonous in God's ear. That does not mean you don't pray for things for a long time. But, to sin in prayer is to turn it into some kind of monotonous *rosary* of sorts.

Rely on the Spirit, praying in the Spirit. Let's consider this just a bit more. Praying in the Spirit is your duty as a Christian. "Behold, he prays." How long does Saul pray? Three days. Three days of prayer and fasting, blinded, before the Lord. It demonstrates humility, faith, love to God, and patience before him. "How many days, Lord must I sit here?" I'm sure echoing in the back of his mind was "you will be told what you must do." Pray until the answer comes. This is by the leading of the Spirit.

"But you, beloved, building yourselves up on your most holy faith, praying in the Holy Spirit, keep yourselves in the love of God, looking for the mercy of our Lord Jesus Christ unto eternal life," (Jude 1:20-21).

Alexander Henderson said, "We must pray "in the Spirit; "that is, we must pray with the heart, sensibly, and not use lip-labor only, for that will not do the trick; but there must be a presenting of the heart, without the which, even without a present heart, our words cannot be free, without wandering here and there."[22] How many people are lip-laborers? Is this what God desires? They say "Father God" a billion times in their prayers, and they do not realize it is a violation of the 3rd commandment!

Praying in the Holy Spirit is where you set your delight on the Almighty God.[23] A hypocrite cannot do that. "Will he delight himself in the Almighty? Will he always call on God?" (Job 27:10). Here you cry Abba Father, by the Spirit of adoption (Gal. 4:5) with childlike affections and confidence boldly coming before the throne of the High Priest Jesus Christ. We will never seek the things above with all our heart, unless we delight in them.

The Spirit of God helps you to pray. The Spirit of God teaches you what you should pray. "We know not what we should pray for as we ought, but the Spirit

---

[22] Henderson, Alexander, *Sermons, Prayers and Pulpit Addresses*, (Coconut Creek, FL: Puritan Publications, 2011), see his sermon on Ephesians 6:14.
[23] "It must be in the Holy Spirit, Jude 1:20, "But ye, beloved, building up yourselves on your most holy faith, praying in the Holy Ghost." He who will speak to God, said St. Ambrose, must speak to him in his own language which he understands, that is, in the language of his Spirit." Watson, Thomas, *The Holy Eucharist, or, the Mystery of the Lord's Supper Briefly Explained*, (Coconut Creek, FL: Puritan Publications, 2012) electronic ed.

maketh intercession for the saints, according to the will of God," (Romans 8:27). Where *is* that will?

Prayer preserves acquaintance with God. It exceedingly quickens the heart; and besides, draws from God new assurances of his love to us, which may serve to kindle our affections towards him. The Spirit removes obstacles to prayer. Nathaniel Vincent said, "he turns that love, that is naturally in the heart to sin, into hatred; he causes the world that was idolized to be condemned; he cures that infidelity, in reference to the excellence of spiritual things, that the unrenewed soul is full of; as also that enmity against God and holiness, which was in the mind all the while it was carnal. "Where the Spirit of the Lord is, there is liberty," (2 Corinthians 3:17), the fetters are knocked off, the clogs removed, the soul is brought out of prison, and is made free, both to the performance of duty, and free in the performance of it."[24]

The Spirit will show you that prayer is better done sooner than later. It is never too late to seek Christ in the power of the Spirit. He will be found by the hearty seeker. Seeking in this way will never be in vain, "But if from thence thou shalt seek the Lord thy God, thou shalt find him, if thou seek him with all thy heart, and with all thy soul," (Deuteronomy 4:29).

The Spirit instructs and teaches us to ask things according to the will of God, lawful and good things. The Spirit of God does not motion you to desire what his word forbids you. And if we pray in the Spirit, the Spirit

---

[24] Vincent, *Spirit of Prayer*, Ibid.

presses us to ask, especially for spiritual blessings. He enables us to pray sincerely and heartily. He enables us to pray with fervency. There we find the Spirit motioning us to zealous prayer. Think about the symbols given to the Spirit in the word that show us how to pray in this zealous way. Fiery tongues. A Mighty Rushing Wind. Seeking. Wrestling with God. The Spirit works fervently in those who are to speak in prayer to God. Such is described as incense, and incense was burnt before it ascended. In such prayers you must cultivate fiery motions of the Spirit. He enables us to pray in faith.

The Spirit molds our prayers to the word, sent to Christ, delivered to the Father by Jesus' intercession. This will be praying "without doubting," (1 Tim. 2:8). *Praying God's word* cannot invite doubting. The word is true, and the word is prayed. God *tends* his word. Faith in this yields to the promises and rests on them. "Whatsoever ye shall ask the Father in my name, he will give it you," (John 14:13). All prayers prayed in this way, according to God's will, are prayers of holiness, given to God by pure hearts that rely on his word. The Spirit's job in part is to make us holy. He does this by the motioning of holy and faithful prayer.

Without the Spirit there is no praying. Those destitute of the Spirit in their natural condition, cannot pray. They may have the ability to pray as the Pharisees, but not in the grace of prayer. In thinking about this pressing into the Kingdom by the Spirit of prayer, can you not see the excellent work prayer is? The whole Trinity works it in you. The Spirit helps us through the word of God to put our requests together. The Son offers them to the Father. The Father accepts them on behalf of Christ's work and intercession. As soon as Paul was converted *he prayed.* In such a thought, then, it should be our wisest action to get the word into our soul, that the Spirit may aid us in praying in the Spirit. We cannot pray without it.

Getting this word into our soul is done under the ministry of the gospel as well as reading and meditating. "Therefore he who supplies the Spirit to you and works miracles among you, does he do it by the works of the law, or by the hearing of faith?" (Gal. 3:5). Sometimes people think that grieving the Spirit is done through some heinous sin. William Jenkyn said, "the Spirit is a delicate thing; do not grieve him by negligence in using his gifts. If the Spirit is gone, your best friend is gone. It was David's prayer, "Take not your Holy Spirit from me." Without the Spirit, you are like hairless Samson, just as another man; poor, weak Samson, when the Lord was departed! You are like a ship that relies on the wind in the sails. There is no stirring without the Spirit's blows. Lord, what were my life if I could not pray! it would even be my burden; and how can I pray without your Spirit?"[25]

---

[25] Jenkyn, William, *An Exposition Upon the Epistle of Jude*, (London: Samuel Holdsworth, 1839), 344.

What is Christ's commentary on *your* devotional life? "Behold, he prays?" As if to justify his work to Ananias in the heart of Saul of Tarsus that murderous Jew, so Christ tells him, consider, this is the magnification of my grace in Saul, "Behold, he prays." What do you think Christ's commentary would be about you if at this very moment he wrote down some important comment about your walk with God? Behold, he watches sports. Behold, he loves to play. Behold, he loves food. Behold, he watches TV. Behold, he loves his ministry. Behold, he loves to be seen by others. Behold, he's knitted to the world. No, no, it should be, "Behold, he prays."

Mark 4: Fasting

One might not think that "fasting" is part of personal devotions, but there is a real need for Christians to cultivate an ongoing hunger for God in the Christian duties of both fasting *and* feasting.

"Moreover *when* ye fast," (Matt. 6:16).

"And he was three days without sight, and neither did eat nor drink," (Acts 9:9).

In the ordination sermon of Jesus for his disciples, we find in Matthew 5-7 the sermon on the mount. Not a sermon in shouting to the people, but a sermon in instructing his disciples. Certainly, people overheard him. But his directives were first to those he was teaching and training. "And seeing the multitudes, He *[that is Jesus]* went up on a mountain, and when he was *seated* his disciples came to him. Then he opened his mouth *and taught them*, saying," (Matt. 5:1-2). If a person goes up on a mountain, he goes there to be secluded. This is not an ideal place to preach from. The people, who were following, would have a hard time hiking a mountain. Now it may be that some followed him. Jesus did not select a podium, or high rock to preach from, as he did on other occasions. As perhaps he did in the sermon on the plain in Luke which covers some of the material found in Matthew in a different manner applied to those listening, yet still with an eye to the apostles. In Luke 6:17ff, we find multitudes around him as he stood to preach, even though Luke records that his *eyes were towards* his disciples. Here, though, on the mountain, he instructed his disciples. Westminster Divine Thomas Hodges said, "The text is a part of Christ's most excellent Sermon on the Mount, (after he had spent a whole night in prayer), to his newly elected Apostles; a kind of ordination sermon."[1]

We find Jesus saying many important and pivotal concepts in this sermon to his disciples. One of those teachings, which, to keep focused, is found in direct conjunction with *prayer*. First he teaches on charity, submission and self-denial. In verses 1-15 he teaches them how to be charitable and then how to pray. In verses 1-4 charitable deeds are to be done secretly. The conclusion of doing charitable deeds is to do them in accordance with the Father's will, which is in secret. God who sees in secret will reward the Christian openly. Likened to this is, then, the reward contained in the act of prayer.

Prayer in secret is also a means of reward done properly. To prayer, in verses 16-18, he then connects *fasting*. "Moreover, when you fast, do not be like the hypocrites, with a sad countenance. For they disfigure their faces that they may appear to men to be fasting. Assuredly, I say to you, they have their reward." *Fasting*

[1] Hodges, Thomas, *The Necessity, Dignity and Duty of Gospel Ministers*, (Crossville, TN: Puritan Publications, 2017) 18.

is to abstain as a religious exercise from food and drink. It is not merely abstinence of food and drink. There is a religious exercise in it.[2] The word "when" is a good translation, though it can have the idea of "whenever you do this." Jesus is, however, quite specific in that it is not "if you fast" but *when* you fast. Fasting is assumed part of the Christian's lifestyle. "But you, when you fast, anoint your head and wash your face, so that you do not appear to men to be fasting, but to your Father who is in the secret place; and your Father who sees in secret will reward you openly," (Matt. 6:16-18). Fasting done in secret has the opportunity of open reward by God. God will openly reward those who in secret pray and fast for spiritual reasons. Fasting is not an act to be done publicly as hypocrites did, like the Pharisees. When *they* fast they want men to consider them as religious, and so they had to look the part of being religious in fasting. Jesus' disciples are forbidden to do this. They are to honor their relationship with God by having a relationship with him in this duty tied to secret prayer. With God's all-seeing eye, that is to be the disciple's aim – pleasing him, not being seen by men.

Consider, now, Acts 9:1-11, Saul, the murderer, converted to Jesus Christ. Saul, later to be named Paul, the murdering hard hearted Pharisee, was threatening believers of the Way, and breathing out threats desiring

---

[2] "I do not call fasting a mere abstinence from meats, but forbearance from sin." Quoting Chrysostom. Du Pin, L.E., *A New History of Ecclesiastical Writers,* (London: Printed for Abel Swalle and Tim. Thilbe 1693) 42.

to kill all those who confessed to be a Christian. In transit to fulfill all his murderous intentions, on his way to Damascus, Saul's miraculous conversion takes place. Christ himself appears to him on the road and regenerates his heart choosing him to be alight to the Gentiles. "So he, trembling and astonished, said, "Lord, what do You want me to do?" Then the Lord said to him, "Arise and go into the city, and you will be told what you must do." Christ appeared for the expressed purpose of converting this murderous wretch to be a preacher and Apostle of Christ's kingdom.

Verse 9 is to be noted: "Then Saul arose from the ground, and when his eyes were opened he saw no one. But they led him by the hand and brought him into Damascus. 9 And he was three days without sight, and neither ate nor drank," (Acts 9:3-9). The moment he was converted, two things occurred which happened simultaneously. He prayed for three days. In the last chapter we covered prayer. But in conjunction with prayer he *fasted* for three days. Saul humbled himself penitently before God upon his conversion in prayer, showing a great evidence of saving faith. Such an evidence was not a short trite prayer. He spent three days praying. He also, though, joined to prayer, fasting. Which, even if just by way of notation, shows that prayer, fasting and repentance are linked together. They are part of the same process of conversion, and they are part of the same Christian lifestyle. Conversion to God, submission to God and self-denial, are accomplished by the Christian to cultivate a hunger and thirst for God alone.

What is fasting? Fasting is a negative act, for a positive outcome. It is vitally linked to humiliation before God. This is something hypocrites have no part in. Hypocrites do not ever look to be humbled in submission to God's will for God's glory and by God's direction.[3] Hypocrites are those pretenders who pretend to try and get into the kingdom of God. Fasting is an open profession of guiltiness before God. It houses in it sorrow and humiliation. It is a true acknowledgment of one's unworthiness, even of the common necessaries of this present life. It houses within it a chastening of the body for the purpose of humiliating the soul before God. If it is merely a healthy fast for bodily good or something of that sort, and then it is tied to the idea of a religious act, it is simply hypocrisy. It must be more than simply bodily exercise. The aim of fasting is that the soul would be *afflicted*. That it would be *humiliated* in God's sight.[4] Afflicting the soul works in the Christian repentance, "for godly sorrow worketh repentance, never to be repented of," (2 Cor. 7:10).

---

[3] "But fasting is a special means to subdue our wanton flesh, and corrupt lusts: for as pampering our bodies adds strength to the old man, so fasting mortifies it, and keeps it down." Gouge, William, *The Whole Armor of God*, (London: John Beale, 1619) 462.
[4] "Fasting is an abstinence from meat and drink undertaken for a time, that the lasciviousness of the flesh may be subdued, and God with the greater fervency may be called upon." Wollebius, John, *The Abridgment of Christian Divinity*, faithfully translated into English by Alexander Ross, (London: T. Mabb for Joseph Nevill, 1660) 339.

Consider first, what fasting is not in religious terms. Fasting is not a human invention. It is commanded by God in various places all through Scripture, as will be noted. Fasting is not famine. When various famines occur throughout history, and people starve, this is not a fast. When people are sick and cannot eat, as with some patients who have something wrong with their throat, for example, this is not a fast. Fasting is not temperance. Temperance in eating is a duty Christians should employ every day. This is so they do not commit the sin of gluttony. Fasting is not the *means* by which a man is made more holy. Holiness is the direct result of the operation of the Spirit not the operation of the human will.[5] Fasting, in and of itself, is also quite useless unless it is tied to the work of the Spirit, and to prayer. Fasting, prayer and the work of the Spirit go together. Fasting is also not something done every day as the three legs to the spiritual chair of personal devotions in bible reading, godly meditation and prayer are to be done. Particular seasons of fasting are determined, then, by providence and circumstance. But make no mistake, fasting is something the wise Christian employs for his good.[6]

---

[5] "For if ye live after the flesh, ye shall die: but if ye through the Spirit do mortify the deeds of the body, ye shall live," (Rom. 8:13).
[6] "An holy fasting may be called a feast,
It feeds the fainting soul, and gives it rest,
He that would gain a life for everlasting
By God's account, is only full with fasting,
A holy hunger doth suppress all evil,
That kind of hunger famisheth the devil."

What is the positive side of fasting. Fasting is a specific form of self-denial before God. It is a putting off of something in this present life which is regularly used for the Christian's life and happiness. Christians do not fast because food is bad. God makes the earth fruitful. Food is a gift, a blessing from God.[7] But fasting is a voluntary putting off of things that are temporary to enflame things that are eternal and spiritual. Fasting is done by denying certain helps and comforts of this life. Fasting is not evil, or bad in that it denies the Christian something. Its motive is to gain something better. It is not a sacrifice of something evil, but of something good. Such self-denial is of good things that are part of the comfort of the Christian, but for a specific spiritual purpose. By itself, it is not a good work and not part of the Christian's obedience toward God, unless it inclines them to make prayer more effective. It is vitally linked to prayer, as it is vitally linked to humility and repentance. Not all Christians, then, will receive the same benefit from this as everyone else. The sanctification of the born again Christian is different in this regard. People are made more holy in different seasons.[8] If the seed of

---

Jordan, Thomas, *Piety, and Poesy,* (London: printed for Robert Wood, 1643) electronic ed.

[7] "He giveth to the beast his food, and to the young ravens which cry," (Psa. 147:9). "The eyes of all wait upon thee; and thou givest them their meat in due season," (Psa. 145:15).

[8] "But he that received seed into the good ground is he that heareth the word, and understandeth it; which also beareth fruit, and bringeth forth, some an hundredfold, some sixty, some thirty," (Matt. 13:23).

regeneration is deposited in the heart of the Christian, sanctification is going to be in varying levels with various people. Fasting's relationship to sanctification is to pull the mind to heaven, which in turn overpowers the body to be called away from those things which are temporary and things pertaining to present-day living. It is conjoined with setting the mind in heaven above where Christ is seated at the right hand of God. It is a holy ordinance given to Christians to see Christ more clearly, and more spiritually effective for sanctifying use.

However, one must also remember that fasting is not always to accompany prayer. Fasting is not for ordinary times of prayer, but for extraordinary times. It is not daily, but employed at specific times. Andrew Willet observes,

> "Fasting is not to accompany ordinary but extraordinary prayer: where must be considered, 1. the occasion of such fasting, which is either in the time of some great judgment and calamity, either to be prevented or else to be removed: or when any special assistance or grace is looked for. 2. The end must be considered, which is not to please God by our fasting, as though it were a part of his service directly, or that we hoped to merit thereby, but only it is used as a means to tame the body and keep it under, to make the inward man more serviceable. Thus the Israelites fasted and prayed, when they had been twice

overcome of Benjamin, entreating the Lords assistance, (Judges 21:1). And see this in Esther in chapter 4, when she was to make a petition for her people. And consider the church of Antioch, when they sent forth Paul and Barnabas to preach, (Acts 13).[9]

There are various kinds of fasting. A natural fast for bodily health which is something a doctor might tell a person if they shouldn't eat red meat anymore. A daily fast that concerns sports. A specific manner of eating, or not eating to produce a certain kind of athlete. These are not what biblical fasting revolves around.

There are various kinds of fasting found in the Bible. These are called *religious* fasts. They are both public and private. The first fast was in the garden of Eden. God told Adam not to eat of the tree of the knowledge of good and evil in Genesis 2:17. The devil, through the serpent in the garden, caused Adam to break this fast and plunged humanity into sin and misery by breaking covenant with God, and as a result, death and the curse came upon all men because all sinned in Adam's transgression. Credited, then, to humanity's account, was the fall and the curse and hell and damnation.[10] Communion with God was interrupted by

---

[9] Willet, Andrew, *Hexapla in Danielem*, (Cambridge: Cantrell Legge, printer to the Vniuersitie of Cambridge, 1610) 361.

[10] "Wherefore, as by one man sin entered into the world, and death by sin; and so death passed upon all men, for that all have sinned," (Rom. 5:12).

interrupting this solemn, covenantal fast. This fast held in place the Covenant of Works, and its violation placed all people for all time under the curse of Adam's fall.[11]

Later, in the Mosaic Law, we find that certain foods were not to be eaten by Israel as a religious theocracy for various reasons. "Nevertheless these you shall not eat among those that chew the cud or those that have cloven hooves," (Lev. 11:4). Biblical fasts are from all manner of food; from bread and water, so far as health will allow (2 Sam. 3:35; Ezra 10:6; Dan. 10:3; Est. 4:16; Acts 9:9). Afflicting the soul is a counterpart of fasting, and that in turn can also be seen in fasting from *things*, like expensive clothes. "For the LORD had said to Moses, "Say to the children of Israel, `You are a stiff-necked people. I could come up into your midst in one moment and consume you. Now therefore, take off your ornaments, that I may know what to do to you,'" (Exod. 33:5). Laying aside things like this from their regular use is a sign of humility and an affliction of the soul. Many of the passages throughout Scripture make this a general part of fasting, in that they wore sackcloth.[12] "My clothing was sackcloth; I humbled myself with fasting; And my prayer would return to my own heart," (Psa. 35:13).

Many people in Scripture fasted from a good night's sleep. "David therefore pleaded with God for the child, and David fasted and went in and lay all night on

---

[11] Rom. 3:23, 5:12.
[12] Esther 4:1-2; Jonah 3:5-6.

the ground," (2 Sam. 12:16). "Gird yourselves and lament, you priests; Wail, you who minister before the altar; Come, lie all night in sackcloth," (Joel 1:13). These can all be seen as extraordinary in comparison to ordinary times of devotion.

Some people in Scripture are directed to fast from pleasure. Husbands and wives for a time are to fast from intimacy, to give themselves to prayer and fasting, (1 Cor. 7:5).

There are various biblical examples of fasts connected directly with prayer in Scripture. Fasting and prayer occasioned public calamities, 2 Samuel 1:12 – when Saul and Jonathan were dead. They surrounded afflictions and sickness, as in Psa. 35:13, where David fasted. They included dangerous and perilous situations, such as Daniel in the lion's den in Dan. 6:18, where we find that Darius fasted. Fasting is connected with approaching danger, as in Esther 4:16 and the eradication of the Jews by Haman. Fasting is linked to the ordination of ministers, "Then, having fasted and prayed, and laid hands on them, they sent them away," (Acts 13:3). This is seen of the disciples, at the time of the consecration of Barnabas and Saul to the ministry. It shows a demonstration of humiliation to God, "And I fell down before the LORD, as at the first, forty days and forty nights; I neither ate bread nor drank water, because of all your sin which you committed in doing wickedly in the sight of the LORD, to provoke Him to anger," (Deut. 9:18). Fasting is linked to understanding the word of God. "You go, therefore, and read from the scroll which you have written at my instruction, the words of the LORD, in the hearing of the people in the LORD'S house on the day of fasting. And you shall also read them in the hearing of all Judah who come from their cities," (Jer. 36:6). And it is the habitual practice by those who professed to love God: by John's disciples, Matt. 9:14; by Anna, Luke 2:37; by Cornelius, Acts 10:30; And by Paul, 2 Cor. 6:5; 11:27. Even hypocrites, who pretend to love God, fasted, such as the Pharisees, (Matt. 9:14; Mark 2:18; Luke 18:12).

The length of fasting varies. It could be prolonged, as it was for three weeks, by Daniel, (Dan. 10:2-3). Forty days by Moses, (Exod. 24:18; 34:28; Deut. 9:9, 18). Forty days by Elijah, (1 Kings 19:8). Both Moses and Elijah, unable to fulfill fasting's *proper* duty, were bested by Jesus Christ the King of glory. In the wilderness, among the assaults and temptations by the devil, there Jesus fasted for forty days *victoriously*, (Matt. 4:2; Mark 1:12-13; Luke 4:1-2).

Fasting is most often used in light of humiliation, repentance and the affliction of the soul. The psalmist does this for himself and his adversaries, (Psa. 109:4, 24). It was seen of Ezra, on account of the idolatrous marriages of the Jews, (Ezra 10:6); of Nehemiah, on account of the desolation of Jerusalem and the temple, (Neh. 1:4); of the Jews, when Jeremiah prophesied against Judea and Jerusalem, (Jer. 36:9); of Daniel, on account of the captivity of the people, with prayer for their deliverance, (Dan. 9:3); of the Ninevites, when Jonah preached to them, (Jonah 3:5–10); and by Paul, at the time of his conversion, (Acts 9:9).

What is the purpose or goal of fasting? It surrounds having more of God than just having things that God can provide; cultivating a hunger *for God*. There are two points to be included here: it surrounds spiritual power and enablement in the Spirit to pray effectively, and it also surrounds the coming of the Kingdom.

Consider fasting in light of spiritual power and enablement in the Spirit. Jesus Christ began his earthly ministry in fasting. What Moses and Elijah, the Law and the Prophets in fasting did not fulfill, Jesus Christ did fulfill by fasting with a perfect aim and a perfect intent. The Jews did not receive with meekness the manna from heaven, living on what God miraculously gives as bread from heaven, showing that man does not live on bread alone but by things which come from God, in fact, the promises and words of he who is faithful (John 6:58).

Paul began his Christian walk with fasting. Every Christian should take time to consider that. Paul engaged in repentance, faith in Christ, prayer and fasting for three days while blind upon his conversion. There are some corruptions and sins which the fall has rendered difficult in Christians. Fasting and prayer help overcome these. These sins and corruptions must be mortified. "Pursue holiness, without which no one will see the Lord," (Heb. 12:14). No holiness, *no eternal life.*

Remaining sin has such a hold on God's people even though converted that Scripture calls them besetting sins,[13] presumptuous sins,[14] even secret faults[15] and they are a great hindrance to sanctification, which, if the Christian is to break them, must be warred on by fasting and prayer with humility, meekness and repentance.[16] Otherwise they will never be overcome. They cannot be completely subdued and conquered except by the power of the Spirit, and the Spirit gives Christians tools to wage war.[17] Two of these weapons of warfare are the spiritual tools of prayer[18] and fasting[19] conjoined. They must be used with the greatest constancy of zeal and strength, because they join together the power of the Spirit in humiliation to destroy the indwelling sin found in the soul.[20] Jesus spoke about the war between the

---

[13] Heb. 12:1.

[14] Psalm 19:13.

[15] Psalm 19:12.

[16] "Fasting, being directed in order to other ends, as for mortifying the body, taking away that fuel which ministers to the flame of lust, or else relating to what is past, when it becomes an instrument of repentance, and a part of that revenge which Paul affirms to be the effect of godly sorrow, is to take its estimate for value, and its rules for practice, by analogy and proportion to those ends to which it does cooperate." Taylor, Jeremiah, *Antiquitates Christianæ, or, The history of the life and death of the holy Jesus as also the lives acts and martyrdoms of his Apostles*, (London: R. Norton for R. Royston 1675) 272.

[17] "... and the sword of the Spirit, which is the word of God," (Eph. 6:17).

[18] Eph. 6:18.

[19] Zech. 8:19; Mark 2:18-20; Luke 5:33, 35.

[20] "Fasting directly advances towards chastity; and by consequence and indirect powers to patience, and humility, and indifference. But then it is not the *fast* of a day that can do this; it is not an act, but a

forces of light and the forces of darkness. "However, this kind does not go out except by prayer and fasting," (Matt. 17:21). This is a desire for spiritual power needed to overcome such things imbedded deep within. Humility in repentance, linked to prayer, and added with fasting, weans the soul away from the world, and causes the affliction of the soul to rely wholly on God's power to sustain. This is more of God, less of man and the world. This is why fasting is called in Scripture, *afflicting the soul.* "Why have we fasted, they say, and You have not seen? Why have we *afflicted* our souls," (Isa. 58:3). It holds in it solemn devotion and worship of God. Tertullian said, "Fasting is a work of reverence towards God."[21] This is cultivating a hunger for him above all things.

Secondly, the coming of the Kingdom of God and fasting are connected. "But the days will come when the bridegroom will be taken away from them, and then they will fast in those days," (Mark 2:20). Be reminded, Jesus said, "When you fast," not *if* you fast. The Lord Jesus explains that when he, the bridegroom is taken away, ascends to heaven, the disciples *will* then fast. Fasting demonstrates to the Christian their intensity and desire for the coming of the Lord. How does one live every day in the end times? Simple, with prayer and fasting until the Lord comes. The cry of the Apostles was, "come Lord

---

state of fasting, that operates to mortification." Emphasis mine. Taylor, Jeremiah, *Antiquitates,* 273.
[21] See Tertullian's work, *De Corona Militis, c. iii.*

Jesus." "He who testifies to these things says, "Surely I am coming quickly." Amen. Even so, come, Lord Jesus!" (Rev. 22:20). The Christian desires Christ's return to judgment to reckon justice upon their enemies and the enemies of the Gospel and to clothe them with white raiment, which is the merit and work of Christ's justifying power visibly enacted for eternity on their very person. Fasting *is an expression of the soul's desire for Christ to return.* Deliverance from the fall, to enter into eternal glory for all time and see the Lamb that sits at the center of eternal bliss is what fasting is centered in. It is, by affliction, a desire looking forward to worshipping God and Christ forever and ever.

Also, as an interesting note, such fasting is also critically attached to preaching. "As they ministered to the Lord and fasted, the Holy Spirit said, "Now separate to Me Barnabas and Saul for the work to which I have called them. Then, having fasted and prayed, and laid hands on them, they sent them away. So, being sent out by the Holy Spirit, they went down to Seleucia, and from there they sailed to Cyprus," (Acts 13:2ff). This is in turn attached to discipleship in the great commission of Matthew 28 of sending preachers to makes disciples. This in turn is attached to the sanctification of the saints who are discipled. This is directly attached to prayer. "Therefore pray the Lord of the harvest to send out laborers into his harvest," (Matt. 9:38). Spiritual power is enabled through fasting as it pertains to the setting apart of preachers to preach the Gospel to the world.

Consider, then, the divine directives of self-denial. Self-denial and self-control are specifically tied to this idea of fasting. Denying of self, and cultivating a hunger for God, as in, "When you fast," (Matt. 6:16). "Draw near to God and he will draw near to you. Cleanse your hands, you sinners; and purify your hearts, you double-minded. Lament and mourn and weep! Let your laughter be turned to mourning and your joy to gloom. Humble yourselves in the sight of the Lord, and he will lift you up," (James 4:8-10). "So likewise, whoever of you does not forsake all that he has cannot be My disciple," (Luke 14:33). Forsaking the world, following Christ and afflicting the soul intertwine. Jesus says a person cannot be his disciple if he does not practice self-denial. "For you were bought at a price; therefore glorify God in your body and in your spirit, which are God's," (1 Cor. 6:20). This is not only religious or spiritual aspects, but an exercise over the body. "But I discipline my body and bring it into subjection" (1 Cor. 9:27), Paul says. The body doesn't inform the mind. The mind ushers control over the body. Gal 5:23 shows "self-control" being a *fruit* of the Spirit. Such is unattainable by the best hypocrites because supernatural spiritual fasting only works through the Spirit.

The content of fasting is always and at every turn in some way tied to bodily sustenance – things the body needs but is denied. Hungering after God is in direct contrast to hungering for physical sustenance. It includes the Christian lowering himself to the duty of self-denial. Saul was murdering Christians, in his own agenda, and when God saved him he was then no more about self, but all about submission and self-denial. "If any man will come after me let him deny himself," Jesus said. No self-denial, well, then you have no part in Christ for fasting cultivates that self-denial.

Fasting is a cultivation of contentment with God and discontentment with the world. Fasting presses the believer to be content in Christ. In other words, *God is enough.* "After these things the word of the LORD came to Abram in a vision, saying, "Do not be afraid, Abram. I am your shield, your exceedingly great reward," (Gen. 15:1). God is the reward. Not grace. Not faith. Not holiness, *per se.* God is the Christian's reward. As with Moses the Christian desires, "Let me see your glory." Man's mind is a factory of idols, and God purges the Christian of those idols of self-love and presses them to be content with Christ alone. "He must increase, I must decrease." God is to be utterly depended on in all things. He is to be for the Christian *his chief good.* Christ is to the Christian the most absolute sovereign who orders all things for the Christian's life by his will and providence. In this the Christian bows in self-denial. No one is allowed, then, by Christ's command, to neglect or dismiss himself from self-denial. Such a one cannot follow Christ without it.

Fasting in self-denial presses the believer to consider being discontent with the fleeting pleasures of the world. Part of this is seen in the proper use of the

Lord's Day which in and of itself is a kind of spiritual fasting. It is putting down the things we like to do the other six days of the week, and focusing on what God wants us to do. We fast from our own pleasures, to take up God's pleasure. "Now godliness with contentment is great gain," (1 Tim. 6:6), especially on the Lord's Day of feasting.

Fleeting pleasures in the world are crucified, and the eye of the afflicted soul looks to Christ for satisfaction and fasting is a help to this. Shall I name all the celebrities and world renown people who seemingly have it all, riches and the like, and there they lie in a coffin, a wooden box as a result of suicide after suicide after suicide? The fleeting pleasures of the world *never* satisfy. The wise Christian must cultivate a hunger *for God,* for the world has nothing to offer them.

Fasting is not "part" of worship, but prepares to arrange and fit the Christian for supernatural worship. It is a *preparative* help. It sends prayers to Christ faster. It chimes louder on supplication and petition. It's like ringing a loud church bell in heaven rather than merely calling God on a cell phone. It gets the Christian there that much faster with more power. If it was part of worship, it would be guided by the *regulative principle* in that it would be specifically outlined, and a means of grace given to everyone in the same way with the same benefits attached. This is not how God set up this work of fasting and self-denial. It is bound to affliction. Weak bodied Christians cannot afflict themselves in this way as those with a stronger constitution. Not everyone can fast for a whole day. It must all be done in prudence.

Fasting is critically attached to prayer. James Ussher, a famous Irish Theologian said, "Unto such extraordinary prayers is annexed a holy fasting or feasting, the one, to further our zeal in petition; the other in thanksgiving."[22] "... for the kingdom of God is not eating and drinking, but righteousness and peace and joy in the Holy Spirit," (Rom. 14:17). Fasting makes prayer more effectual. "The effective, fervent prayer of a righteous man avails much," (James 5:16); add *fasting* to that. It's like putting nitric (that explosive gas) into a race car to make it run faster. Yet, only for a short period of time.

Christians ought to see the link between prayer and fasting as a means to greater sanctification and spiritual power in a shorter period. During the great awakening, Jonathan Edwards said, "I should think the people of God in this land, at such a time as this is, would be in the way of their duty, to do three times so much at fasting and prayer as they do."[23] This is so the whole man may be more humbled before God, and more fervent in prayer. Throw a little nitric on those prayers while the glory is pouring out by the Spirit's providence. Don't take your foot off the gas now; it is the time the Christian must put the peddle to the metal. To keep the benefit

[22] Ussher, James, *A Body of Divinity*, (London: R.B. Seely and W. Burnside: 1841) 458.
[23] Edwards, Jonathan, *The Great Awakening*, Volume 4, (New Haven; London: Yale University Press, 2009) 516.

flowing in the Spirit's power. As Jesus taught as it relates to spiritual power and work in the kingdom (and in this case demonic possession and exorcism in his day), "However, this kind does not go out except by prayer and fasting," (Matt. 17:21). "This kind can come out by nothing but prayer and fasting," (Mark 9:29). There is enhanced spiritual power attached to prayer when fasting is joined together to it.

There are myriads of biblical examples of fasting and prayer linked together. Ezra, "So we fasted and entreated our God for this, and he answered our prayer," (Ezra 8:23). David, "My clothing was sackcloth; I humbled myself with fasting; and my prayer would return to my own heart," (Psa. 35:13). Daniel, "Then I set my face toward the Lord God to make request by prayer and supplications, with fasting, sackcloth, and ashes," (Dan. 9:3). Paul, "that you may give yourselves to fasting and prayer," (1 Cor. 7:5).

One of the best evidences of the converted Christian is secret fasting and prayer. Robert Leighton said, "Fasting, which is a necessary help of Prayer, unclogs and frees the wings of the soul to fly to heaven."[24] John Brinsley called fasting *the feathers glued onto the arrow to allow it to hit its mark.*

---

[24] Leighton, Robert, *The Whole Works of Robert Leighton*, Volume 3, (London: Hatchard and Son, 1830) 48. Thomas Grenfield also said fasting, "unclogs the soul, and takes off that mire and dirt that hangs about the wings of the mind, whereby it mounts much higher in all spiritual acts." *The fast: As it was delivered in a sermon at St. Margarets in Westminster, before the honorable House of*

Your spiritual duties, needs, trials, and such, are consecrated by fasting and prayer. Spiritual duties are enhanced by cultivating a reliance on God, a hunger for Christ, *instead* of merely a hunger for pizza. But they are not instantaneously enhanced. God does not operate grace in that way that all are instantly changed. It happens in degrees. Can the hypocrite do this? Will he? Can he pray always and accompany times of prayer with fasting? He can hardly pray. He will never put up with it. When he prays, if he prays at all, and answers don't come as he likes, he leaves off praying. The Christian *adds* to praying, fasting, to get those answers because true Christians are serious about cultivating a hunger for God. In this way we ought eagerly and constantly to persevere in our godly desires, until they are fully satisfied, or else we are hypocrites.

Why add fasting to prayer? Why does God do that? Why the need for more spiritual power, a subject of self-denial and submission to him? Why not just sanctify us upon our request? A true desire fulfilled...why not? It is used to keep us in a perpetual humble subjection and dependence on him. He does not grant everything in answering prayer, ever, *all at once*. He leads us along, by yielding a little and a little, so that he may *keep us* in a humble dependence on him. *Thy kingdom come*, we pray, now, but still, it is *not yet*.

Commons upon Wednesday the 12th. of June 1661. (London: Printed for Henry Brome at the Gun in Ivy-lane) 7.

Scripture does not give a specific time to fast, but allows you to discern when it should be employed. Maybe it is for pardon of some sin. Maybe overcoming a besetting sin you struggle with. Maybe looking to be more than an awakened sinner, but a converted saint. Maybe to look to discern what secret faults you don't even know you do. David prayed that.[25] Maybe there is a certain special spiritual blessing needed that you believe you lack. Richard Sibbes said, "There are some kinds of miseries, some kind of calamities, some kind of sins, that will not be overcome, and which God will not deliver the church from, but by fasting and prayer."[26] Maybe it's just that you desire God more than everything else and want to cultivate a greater hunger for him. You desire to see Christ's return and see the eternal age ushered in. Fasting will never bring you to heaven, but it will, through the earnestness of the saints, be a means to bring heaven down to you, at least for a time. You hunger for God rather than the delicacies laid out by the world. Consider days that you fast as days of sanctification. Set apart times to afflict your souls before God in fasting and prayer, and *deny self.* Fasting is really "heart work." "Labor to afflict your souls for sin; meet God with weeping and supplication; clothe yourselves with humility, lie in the dust, cover yourselves with shame; loathe and abhor yourselves in his sight for your

---

[25] "Who can understand his errors? cleanse thou me from secret faults," (Psa. 19:12).
[26] Sibbes, Richard, *The Works of Richard Sibbes,* Volume 3, (Edinburgh: Banner of Truth Trust, 1982), 187.

iniquities, mourn for your own sins, and for the great dishonors of his Name by the sins of others. And seek the Lord, both for yourselves, and for his church."[27] That's heavy, but often, and especially in our age, necessary.

Sometimes you are forced into a fast by God through trials. Such trials and difficulties will quicken you into duties. Sometimes maybe special meditation. Sometimes it might be for special study. Sometimes it is for discernment to understand his providence. But it is especially powerful when joined one with another, fasting *and* prayer. Yet, we must have repentance first, before fasting and prayer in this way will ever be acceptable. Repentance casts all cares on Christ and God. It acknowledges your reliance on him. Fasting flames that fire.

When do *you* fast and pray? When was the last time you did so? The Pharisees fasted and prayed once a week, but from a wrong heart. You must do more than the hypocrite can do. The hypocrite does many strenuous religious exercises. They read, pray, fast, are found in church, seem to be Christians, but they do things from a wrong motive, not self-denial, but of vain-glory. "I fast twice a week; I give tithes of all that I possess," (Luke 18:12). How do you compare to them, and they are those who are wayward and as Christ said

---

[27] Vincent, Thomas, *The Way to Escape the Horrible and Eternal Burnings of Hell Through Jesus Christ*, (Coconut Creek, FL: Puritan Publications, 2012) 154.

will receive greater condemnation.[28] The Christian must always do more than the hypocrite does.

How does your fasting measure up to your feasting? We love to eat. One friend said "life is food." Everything happens around the dinner table. We have whole channels on TV that cater to food, no pun intended. The Food Channel. The Cooking Channel. News Feeds always have a *food* section. As much as we feast, we should also consider the fast, and instead feast on God's fat and marrow.[29]

There is a preparation to fast and pray. There are two aspects to this preparation that you have to consider. First, the actual consideration *of* fasting and prayer. Second, considering what *God wants you to do.*

Fasting needs thought. You have to know why you fast in order to fast well. What is your end of fasting? What is your need to do it? How can you best do it so it glorifies God the most, and is beneficial to you most? Keep it in mind, you are putting off the world to gain more of God, and to make your prayers more effectual for the "thing" you need or desire. You must think that through.

What does God want you to do? He wants you to humble yourself. Humility pleases the sovereign God.

---

[28] "Woe unto you, scribes and Pharisees, hypocrites! for ye devour widows' houses, and for a pretence make long prayers: therefore ye shall receive the greater damnation," (Matt. 23:14).

[29] "And in this mountain shall the LORD of hosts make unto all people a feast of fat things, a feast of wines on the lees, of fat things full of marrow, of wines on the lees well refined," (Isa. 25:6).

He looks on, as Isaiah 66:2 says, those who are, "poor and of a contrite spirit..." Jesus said that such people are blessed, "blessed are those who mourn." He wants you to succeed in the act. That means plan ahead. Things commonly dealt with in the world need to be thought about so you don't stumble in your fast. Don't fast when you go on vacation. He wants you to have a ready mind and heart to succeed. Tobias Crisp said, "Our spirits are like wild heifers to any service, especially to such a self-fomenting exercise, as a fast; they will be rising and kicking even at the fore-thought of it, and grumble at the tediousness of it; and certainly we shall find them very sullen and lifeless at it, if we do not provoke our souls to it before hand."[30] We tend to turn it into a negative work all around, where it really is negatively done, but a positive work for our soul. Be resolved to complete the work. Resolutions are exceedingly important. One of Jonathan Edwards' *Resolutions* that he read weekly, was this: #20 Resolved, to maintain the strictest temperance in eating and drinking. He did this as if preparing every day for the coming fast. Earnestly pray that Christ will send his Spirit to you to quicken your spirit in the work, and receive the needed strength to overcome any hindrances.

How should you start fasting? First, consider what your reason is for fasting, in light of sanctification. It's always going to first surround being starved for

---

[30] Crisp, Tobias, *The Complete Works of Tobias Crisp*, Volume 2, (London: Printed for John Bennett, 1832) 381.

Christ. You want more of Jesus Christ. You want more of the bridegroom. You want to see him face to face. "I will rise now," I said, "And go about the city; In the streets and in the squares I will seek the one I love," (Song of Songs 3:2). Colossians 3 speaks to this strategy. "If then you were raised with Christ, seek those things which are above, where Christ is, sitting at the right hand of God. Set your mind on things above, not on things on the earth. For you died, and your life is hidden with Christ in God. When Christ who is our life appears, then you also will appear with Him in glory," (Col. 3:1-4). As a Christian, you should hunger and thirst after righteousness in Christ more than after bread or drink. God says to you, "Love me above all things." *Hunger* after me. You are to look to Christ as the only chief good; the first and best of beings and the place where you hunger and thirst will be satisfied. Jesus promises if you do that, you will be filled. Christ alone is where all your happiness resides. It is as if he was to say, "Seek me, Christian, above all; and nothing besides me." Fasting and prayer in humility and meekness cast you wholly on him where you do not regard anything more valuable in the world, even as it relates to your life. God has given himself to you to enjoy. What is meat and drink compared to him? He is the true feast.

Second, start simple and easy. Begin by fasting from one meal in a week, and then consider what you will specifically put in the place of that meal in your prayer time. Take the time you would have eaten, to pray, study and meditate on the word. "Every word that comes from the mouth of God." Plan *that* out. Occupy that time with some spiritual benefit. Without that plan, its not fasting but just starving. Then, after a time, do this for two meals. Later, do this for three meals, and maybe choose to drink juice, or something like that, for the day. Wind up, at last, having a fast day.

Third, fasting is linked to prayer so fasting is not something you do as a single act. You do not *just* fast, ever. You fast from food, and fill up with the word. Man does not live by bread alone...he lives by every word that God has given him in the word. Link fasting to these other disciplines so that it may be effective and you will see a great reaping of reward in the end.

There *is* a reward in fasting. It is the removal of strong corruptions and sins, among other benefits. Christians look to kill sin to be conformed to the image of God. Hypocrites ask for forgiveness without ever doing anything to kill that which they seem to want to be delivered from. Confession is not supplication. There are some corruptions and vices, besetting sins for example, that are strongly set in you as remaining sin, in some part by habit, and these hold you in place discouraging the work of killing sin to a further degree. With prayer, fasting is a conduit by which the Spirit of God works a greater and more effective spiritual power to overcome those more difficult embedded sins. Like the demon that only comes out by prayer and fasting because it is was so deeply rooted.

There is the removal of possible judgment by God. One of the most fearful verses in Scripture is God abandoning the means of grace to make it effectual for his people. "Ephraim is joined to idols, let him alone," (Hos. 4:17). God leaves the sinner in his sin and the sinner has no idea that God has left. Repentance first, fasting second, lest God take away the effectual nature of the word, as he has in so many nominal churches around the globe.

There are heights of new grace found. The soul in this world is never fully satisfied with the good things of God until it is in heaven. This life is a life filled with desires and longing. The church, though, is connected to Christ in this world, but the finality of the marriage will be in heaven. That means as a Christian, your desires are still for further and further communion with Christ in his ordinances here, but forever in heaven. You seek for new grace each week. To be brought greater in religion this week than you were the week before. Why? Because you seek more of Christ, and more of grace.

"... and your Father who sees in secret will reward you openly," (Matt. 6:18). Why will God reward you if you fast in secret? Why does he reward fasting at all? Why will he reward you at all? Do you expect a reward? Christians certainly do – cultivating a greater hunger for God. They find more of God in his ordinances because God is there in all of them. *God* is your reward.

Fasting and prayer, to keep them linked, is not something accomplished in your own will. You don't do some spiritual work in your own strength, and then expect God to pay you what is due. Your fruit is the Spirit working through you. "But the fruit of the Spirit is longsuffering, faithfulness, *self-control*," (Gal. 5:22-23). Who's fruit? The Spirit's fruit. You don't want your prayer and fasting to be done begrudgingly, nor as some work you do like the Pharisees did thinking then that God owes you something. Such a thing, Romans 4 tells us, is a "debt owed." And, you must be sure to remember that when you think you should be owed some reward for doing your duty, even the best duties you have are tainted with sin. And God requires all duties to be perfect. What then, will he reward? "... for it is God who works in you both to will and to do for his good pleasure," (Phil. 2:13). God works religious fasting and prayer that honors him through you for his glory. God rewards you because you are weak (not that you *should* be). "For when I am weak, then I am strong," (2 Cor. 12:10). "... that in all things God may be glorified through Jesus Christ, to whom belong the glory and the dominion forever and ever," (1 Peter 4:11). One preacher said, "Fasting is an offering of emptiness to God in hope." But that is incomplete. Fasting is an offering of emptiness to God in hope that God will fill you up in Jesus Christ for his glory. Nothing else can satisfy you like Christ can. You are to be satisfied in God, giving him all the glory amidst the affliction of your soul. That is the glory Christ receives from those who cultivate a hunger for God.

Mark 5: Family Worship Part 1

"For I know him, that he will command his children and his household after him, and they shall keep the way of the LORD, to do justice and judgment; that the LORD may bring upon Abraham that which he hath spoken of him," (Gen. 18:19).

In Genesis 18:1-15 is found the narrative of Abraham, the righteous prophet. Abraham is visited by three angels in 18:1-15. In recalling the narrative, God sets forth a promise to Abraham and Sarah that they will indeed have the promised blessing of Isaac. It will not be a child outside the line and lineage of the woman. It will not be Ishmael. Abraham shows hospitality to the Angels, initially not knowing it was the pre-incarnate Christ, the Angel of the Lord, speaking with him. At the point which two angels leave to go to Sodom and Gomorrah for their destruction, it is revealed that Abraham is speaking with God.

The angelic visitors leave Abraham and the Lord speaks (verses 16-22). God begins to address Abraham to inform him of what he is about to do. Abraham is the *father of nations* and since God is going to take one of these nations away, he informs Abraham why he will not be its father. Sodom and Gomorrah are wicked and will be destroyed.

God says he *knows* Abraham in this discourse. The meaning is that God has "chosen him." Literally *known him from among all the families of the earth.* The use of the Hebrew word "to know" is used throughout the Old Testament in the sense to "choose." "You only have I known of all the families of the earth," (Amos. 3:2). "But since then there has not arisen in Israel a prophet like Moses, whom the LORD knew face to face," (Deut. 34:10). "Now what more can David say to You? For You, Lord GOD, know Your servant," (2 Sam. 7:20). In electing Abraham, and *knowing* him, here the ground of election was God's promise to Abraham.

The church often neglects to take God at his word. God told Abraham, "I will be a God to you and your children after you," and this is a promise to him. Abraham believed this and it was credited to him for righteousness. Yet, this electing knowledge of God, this electing love of God, to Abraham in verse 18, its fuller purpose, is now stated for the first time. "For I have known him, in order that he may command his children and his household after him, that they keep the way of the LORD, to do righteousness and justice, that the LORD may bring to Abraham what he has spoken to him," (Gen. 18:19). God desires to see in his elect servant a God-fearing household in opposition to the nation he is about to destroy.

In Genesis 17:11 the future obligation placed on Abraham's descendants appeared to be limited to the duty of circumcision. "This is My covenant which you shall keep, between Me and you and your descendants after you: Every male child among you shall be circumcised; and you shall be circumcised in the flesh of your foreskins, and it shall be a sign of the covenant between Me and you," (Gen. 17:10-11). First, there is the sign of being chosen, and then comes the command to improve that sign – a godly and instructed household.

In Gen. 18:19 Abraham is told to do a number of religious exercises in his home. He is to command his children. The future generations of the covenant promise. He is to *command* his household. This would include his wife, which is an interesting thought. This also includes all his household workers. Abraham is instructed by God, to further instruct his whole household. Abraham is to teach them that they keep the way of the LORD. The way of peace. The way of happiness. The way of salvation. In a word, the way of the everlasting covenant. Covenant families in this regard are taught to do righteousness and justice. For what reason? So that the promises extended to Abraham, promised to him, would indeed be fulfilled and come to pass to the future seed. And, all this is accomplished by the Lord, that the Lord may bring to Abraham what he has spoken to him. If he is to act like a pagan, then the promises don't fit. Only righteous households that execute justice in the sight of God, walking in his ways are fit to receive the benefits of his promises.

The obligation of instructing children, family and household is constantly reiterated from this point forward throughout Scripture.[1] God was and is very concerned with whole households. This is why you find *household* baptisms in Acts. Household is a Hebraism even in the New Testament where everyone in the house was included. "Now a certain woman named Lydia heard us. She was a seller of purple from the city of Thyatira, who worshiped God. The Lord opened her heart to heed the things spoken by Paul. And when she and her household were baptized ..." (Act. 16:14-15). The promise was made and executed to Abraham, and it was his responsibility to usher his home into the hands of Christ and into other households. Lydia was a recipient of this promise to Abraham.

In the law, prophets, wisdom literature, *etc.*, this concept is found in numerous instances. "It will come to pass when you come to the land which the LORD will give you, just as he promised, that you shall keep this service. "And it shall be, when your children say to you, What do you mean by this service?' "that you shall say, It is the Passover sacrifice of the LORD, who passed over the houses of the children of Israel in Egypt when he struck the Egyptians and delivered our households." So the people bowed their heads and worshiped," (Exod. 12:25-27). This is catechizing in the home. "And these

---

[1] "No minister is more straightly charged of God, to teach and catechize his flock, then you are to instruct your children. Parents stand obliged to their children, by more and stronger bonds, then any Pastor can be to his flock." Hildersham, Arthur, *CLII lectures Upon Psalm 51,* (London: George Miller for Edward Brewster, 1635) 289.

words which I command you today shall be in your heart. "You shall teach them diligently to your children, and shall talk of them when you sit in your house, when you walk by the way, when you lie down, and when you rise up," (Deut. 6:6-7). "My son, hear the instruction of your father, And do not forsake the law of your mother," (Prov. 1:8). In Job 23:11, observing the LORD's way is equated with observing his commands. And Job regularly engaged his household (1:15) in religious exercises. In Psalm 18:22 such teaching is identified with doing "righteousness." Abraham, being *known by God,* knows God *back*, and has a unique responsibility to commit to his household the ways of God. This stands in direct contrast to the actions of Sodom and Gomorrah which were cities that indulged in idolatry of self, homosexual sensuality and heinous sin. Abraham is to teach righteousness and justice to his household. Righteousness revolves around the Hebrew idea of making decisions according to God's truth without partiality.[2] Abraham is to know God's truth. He is to impart that truth to his family. Justice is an outworking of righteousness. When righteousness is executed, justice results. Justice is the practical application of what Abraham knows to be true and right according to the character and will of God. He is to teach that to his family. God tells Him this in preface to what he is about

---

[2] "Hear me when I call, O God of my righteousness," (Psa. 4:1). "He restoreth my soul: he leadeth me in the paths of righteousness for his name's sake," (Psa. 23:3).

to reveal about the nation of Sodom and Gomorrah. Their sin has hit its mark, and God is now going to destroy them in a righteous act of justice. The outcry of Sodom is great; to "cry" means that God has taken notice of the situation. A "cry" which comes up to the face of God. "Their sin is very great" means *severe and heavy, exceedingly intense.* John Calvin commented on the sin of Sodom when he said, "But when we perceive that the anger of God is provoked by the sin of man, men should be inspired with a dread towards sinning."[3] Sodom was not.

Verse 21 is very reminiscent of the narrative in Genesis 11 of the tower of Babel, where God "went down" to look. God says he will go down to see, and if it is, he will know. "I will go down now and see whether they have done altogether according to the outcry against it that has come to Me; and if not, I will know," (Gen. 18:21). Does God know everything? Certainly. Why then does he say this? It's known that God already has planned to destroy Sodom. This is seen in Gen. 19:13 where the angels say they have come to destroy it and they were already gone when Abraham began talking with God in his barter for the cities in verse 22ff. But God uses this time to work Abraham into a situation to outwardly demonstrate to his chosen and elect servant whether or not what he already expects of him will be the case – to be a teacher of righteousness and justice one must be righteous and just in their conversation.

---

[3] Calvin, *Institutes*, 3:21:3.

When I use the word, "conversation", this is not meant simply in Abraham's conversation in speaking with God, but in the conversation or carrying of one's self in the world while he lives in it. Abraham was to teach his family all about this.

DOCTRINE: God's people have the unique responsibility to commit to their household the instruction of the righteousness and justice of God.

The word *justice*, or *righteousness*, is used in Scripture in a moral sense to mean "right." The Hebrew idea behind speaking of God's righteousness is speaking of God's "rightness."[4] The purity of his actions, which points to his knowledge and its outworking, is his *rightness*. The Greek idea in the New Testament links that idea with its negation of, "missing the mark."[5] When someone misses the mark, or sins, they are being *un-righteous*. When men conform to what is right in a moral sense they imitate God.[6] God is a righteous Ruler who has Laws that are holy, just and good.[7] God faithfully adheres to those Laws as consistent with his

---

[4] "Thy righteousness also, O God, is very high, who hast done great things: O God, who is like unto thee!" (Psa. 71:19). "In his days Judah shall be saved, and Israel shall dwell safely: and this is his name whereby he shall be called, THE LORD OUR RIGHTEOUSNESS," (Jer. 23:6).
[5] "That as sin hath reigned unto death, even so might grace reign through righteousness unto eternal life by Jesus Christ our Lord," (Rom. 5:21). "Awake to righteousness, and sin not," (1 Cor. 15:34). "For he hath made him to be sin for us, who knew no sin; that we might be made the righteousness of God in him," (2 Cor. 5:21).
[6] "Be ye therefore followers of God, as dear children," (Eph. 5:1).
[7] "Wherefore the law is holy, and the commandment holy, and just, and good," (Rom. 7:12).

nature and character. This consistency is found in his word, and especially in his law. The moral law is a mirror of God's character. If a person keeps the law perfectly, they will act like God acts. If they do not keep the law, once the law is exposed to them, they know what sin is, as Paul illustrates in Romans 6-7. The problem is that through Adam's sin in the garden which cursed all men, keeping the moral law perfectly is impossible. Yet, God doesn't change his character to suit men's nature. Men are still obliged to act righteously and with all manner of justice. Even though they are fallen, they are to seek to shun evil and do good no matter what. God judges men in light of this.

God judges everything according to his nature, and according to his holiness. "God is a righteous judge," (Psa. 7:11). "He shall judge the world with righteousness," (Psa. 96:13). The Psalmist also writes, "Clouds and darkness are round about Him: righteousness and judgment are the habitation of his throne," (Psa. 97:2). God is a moral being, and from his righteousness flows various attributes which grow out of his moral character. This is why God requires Abraham to teach his children and household about his moral character. Teach them *about him*.

Having stated that in brief, such righteousness is to be taught to the family, we look to call this instruction of the household, family worship, or family instruction.[8]

---

[8] "And all of you labour now to instruct your children in the knowledge of God and of Christ, bring them up in the fear of the

It is done at the family altar, metaphorically called this under these times of the Gospel. It is a metaphorical emblem of family worship. In the priesthood of all believers, the family worships at the family altar. They make sacrifices to God there in prayer, praise, instruction, conversation, reading and such.

Family worship is biblically necessary. It is biblically necessary to show that one's household is of the faith of Christ's people, of the spiritual lineage of Abraham. It is biblically necessary of the household or family if they are going to serve God as God requires righteously.

What is family worship? Generally speaking, God is to be worshipped by all, which includes the family. Abraham was instructed to command his household, his children, his family and even those who worked for him. How did he do this? By both precept and pattern. By precept, Gen. 18:19, "For I know him, that he will command his children and his household after him, and they shall keep the way of the LORD, to do justice and judgment; that the LORD may bring upon Abraham that which he hath spoken of him." Abraham instructed his family on things he knew, based on what God said in instructing him and that he learned as a result. So, he taught them by word of mouth. Christians are to show others in their family what is to be said in

---

Lord that they may be seed for that day." Burroughs, Jeremiah, *An Exposition of the Prophesy of Hosea* (London: Printed for R. Dawlman, 1652) 143.

God's behalf. They are to be commended in religion to them, to be disparaged in the way of sin and of the world; they are to be bound to godly duty, and oblige them by the authority that federal household governors have over them.

Interestingly, people also learn by pattern. It is never *do what I say not what I do.* They must see the walk. They are to be aware of bad examples that might be given before their eyes. Thomas Boston said, for he that sins before a child, sins twice; for his sin lies fair to be repeated by the young spectator.[9]

A Christian's strength is spiritual, 1 Sam. 2:9, "By strength shall no man prevail." The one who succeeds is the one who does so by God's appointed means. For God is never in those things not appointed by him. By prayer all these things are anointed. Any success is the Lord's doing, so it is necessary that Christians pray for those at the throne of grace who are within their house. The mission field is first at home. Psalm 66:4 says, "All the earth shall worship You and sing praises to You." This includes the family. As a matter of fact, it is directed to the family in a subtle manner since all the earth is made up of family units.

Family worship is the combined worship given to God by all the members of one household. Families have always worshipped God. This is found all through

---

[9] Boston, Thomas, *The Complete Works of Thomas Boston*, Volume 5, (Wheaton: Richard Owen Roberts Publishers, 1980) 612.

the Bible.[10] Altars (Num. 7:84) were said to be dedicated when they were set apart for God's service, and consecrated for that use. Esther and the maids of her house, and the rest of the Jews in their several families, fasted and prayed (Esther 9:31). Such worship is spoken of by the prophets. "And the land shall mourn, every family by itself," (Zech. 12:12). Cain and Abel worshipped at the altar (Gen. 4). Noah worshipped by the altar; he even did this with his family upon the exit from the ark after the flood (Gen. 8:20). Family worship is not only by precept but also by pattern. It is not only by command but by example. Abraham was given a promise of blessing annexed to it. And once some of the catechistic passages are added to it, its constant employment is seen. "You shall teach them diligently to your children, and shall talk of them when you sit in your house, when you walk by the way, when you lie down, and when you rise up," (Deut. 6:7). This is echoed again in 11:18-19. It's written on the very posts of their house to signify what kind of house it is and what one will find inside. Job, in that ancient text and book, had a great religious care of his family. Job 1:5, "So it was, when the days of feasting had run their course, that Job would send and sanctify them, and he would rise early in the morning and offer burnt offerings according to the number of them all. For Job said, "It may be that my sons have sinned and cursed God in their hearts." Thus Job did regularly."" In relation to ordinances, God directs

---

[10] Gen. 4, 18; Exod. 12; Deut. 6; Joshua 24; Job 1; Psa. 30, 101, *etc.*

families to partake of them, "Speak to all the congregation of Israel, saying: On the tenth day of this month every man shall take for himself a lamb, according to the house of his father, a lamb for a household," (Exod. 12:3). Oliver Heywood said, "This was for every individual family, and person, and it must be every day, not only on Sabbath days, and other solemnities, but it shows that God must be daily worshipped; yes, it must be morning and evening, that prayer and praise may be the lock and key of the day."[11] Joshua 24:15 is another key text to follow, "But as for me and my house, we will serve the LORD." Service to God is accomplished by the whole house. "At the same time," says the LORD, "I will be the God of all the families of Israel, and they shall be My people," (Jer. 31:1). Even in speaking generally about his own teachings, Jesus Christ set instruction in the midst of the family. Matthew 12:50, "For whoever does the will of My Father in heaven is My brother and sister and mother." It demonstrated a relationship that was family oriented. In Acts 10:1-2 Cornelius had a house devoted to God, "There was a certain man in Caesarea called Cornelius, a centurion of the band called the Italian band, a devout man, and one that feared God with all his house." How did his house do that? Part time? Lois and Eunice are mentioned in 2 Timothy 1:5 the primary influence on Pastor Timothy through the Scriptures. It is impossible to make the argument that the family unit

---

[11] Heywood, Oliver, *The Works of Oliver Heywood*, Volume 4, (Edinburgh: John Vint, 1827) 314.

should not worship if God expects worship from all. Joshua's service to God is not done once a week for an hour; it's not part time. Service to God, to use Job's description, was regular, and *continual.* And it is no wonder that God singles Job out as one who fears God (worships and shuns evil). This is the very thing Joshua tells the Israelites to do – serve God and forsake idols. Elders or pastors are even measured in this for their office. To neglect the instruction of the family is a non-negotiable disqualification for a man from the office. They are to be ruling their own houses well (1 Tim. 3:4, Titus 1:6). They cannot rule God's house without ruling their house well. And what is it to rule God's house? It's teaching people the Scriptures; it is instruction.

Family worship will induce the reformation of the family in understanding the righteousness of God through Christ. This is God's means by which he will transform the character and disposition of those in the family. In God's covenant promises, there are blessings and promises to families. Abraham's whole family was in covenant (Gen. 17). Lydia's whole family was baptized in covenant. Cornelius' house, Joshua's house, the jailor's house, *etc.* Yet, such teaching and leading come first with a single person before it can affect the family. Abraham as the federal head in his covenant relationship with God, or God appointed representative of his family, was first affected by following and serving God. Only by his action to serve God can he, with any great solemnity, cause his family to joyfully serve God as well and to learn righteousness and justice. Underscore the word *joyfully*. It only takes one obedient individual to affect others in this way. But it must start with someone. One preserver, one salty person, will preserve and affect others in a godly manner. Such a one will lead others into joy before God.[12]

  Who is it that leads family worship? It is the one who leads the family. Not everyone, obviously, is a bible scholar. The Scriptures place the responsibility of family worship on the head of the family. This is given to the federal head of the family (the father or husband should lead their families to godly reform as the representative of his household in covenant with God). Unless the head of the household is an ungodly man, the federal head should lead the family in family devotions. God has given the federal headship to the man, who is the head of the women and the instructor of the family. There is no passage in scripture that says "If he can't teach then he should abdicate his duties to his wife, or to some other person." Every head of household can read the bible,

---

[12] "God is not only to be worshipped alone in a family, but jointly and together. For every Christian family should be a little Church; like that, Rom. 16:5. Now it's not enough, that the members of the Church worship God alone, but it ought to be done together, the same reason holds in a family; namely, for mutual edification, that the stronger may help the weaker, and that all may worship without fail. It is also much for the honor of God, that many join in his service. And the very tenor of that pattern of prayer, Matt. 6:11. runs plural, "Our Father, which art in Heaven." And proves besides, that daily prayer ought to be used by diverse people together, "Give us this day our daily bread." Steele, Richard, *The Husbandman's Calling*, (London: M.S. and are to be sold by E. Calvert, 1668) 269-270.

pray and talk with their family about the Lord's Day sermon. If that head of household is negligent, such a family will be in a low degree of having high thoughts of God. It is the father's responsibility to lead his family before God, or as Joshua said he would do, "serve God," or as God commanded Abraham, to teach righteousness and justice to his children and household.

Think about the effect that the family altar has on the family. First, its commanded by God to worship in this way. Second, it has a direct propensity to make godliness and religion a matter of interest every day. Third, it should be a daily activity, then it is expected and becomes part of the family régime. The things of God should be the predominant influence in any Christian home, and this happens by way of family worship and the family altar. Matthew Henry said, "Our houses must be churches; with ourselves we must give up our houses to the Lord, to be to Him for a name and a people."[13]

The 1647 Westminster Directory of Private Worship has much to say on family worship. First, they cover individuals who are faithful in their devotions before God. Bible reading, bible study, godly meditation, and prayer are all included in this. Second, they show

---

[13] "Blessed be God, there is a way of sanctifying our houses to be holy unto the Lord, without either selling them or buying them. If we and our houses serve the Lord, if religion rule in them, and we put away iniquity far from them, and have a church in our house, holiness to the Lord is written upon it, it is his, and he will dwell with us in it." Henry, Matthew, *Matthew Henry's Commentary on the Whole Bible*, (Peabody, MA: Hendrickson, 1994) 186.

what three important areas the family should exercise private worship. They label the first, *Prayer and Praises.* Prayers should be made for the church, for the country, for the family and for specific members of the family. Next, *Reading of the scriptures.* Next, *catechizing* in a plain way, that the understandings of the simpler may be the better enabled to profit under the public ordinances, and they made more capable to understand the scriptures when they are read. Yes, the reason for catechizing is to teach righteousness and justice to the children and family, but it also is used, as stated, to profit under the public ordinances of the church, which is for the benefit of worship, preaching, the Lord's Supper and the like. The more one is taught, the more they will profit from worship in church. Where grace is dispensed through preaching so hearing and faith can take place.

Added to this is also Scriptural discussion: together with godly conferences tending to the edification of all the members in the most holy faith: as also, admonition and rebuke, upon just reasons, from those who have authority in the family. Both discussing Scripture, theology or the like, is expected. Also, in its application to the family, some may need to be reproved for sin, or such. Added to this, a warning is given. The head of the family is to take care that none of the family withdraw himself from any part of family-worship: and, seeing the ordinary performance of all the parts of family-worship belongs properly to the head of the family, the minister is to stir up such as are lazy, and train up such as are weak, to a fitness to these exercises. The reason they give for all this, is that such things commanded by God which press the family to godliness will be "cherished".

God uses the family altar of worship for the good of his people and the good the church;[14] it promotes reformation and ultimately readies families for revival. Families have the unique responsibility to commit to their household the instruction of the righteousness and justice of God. Such will teach their families the path of righteousness. Who knows what blessing will come from such things in God's time?

God discriminates between two kinds of families – those that worship him and those that do not. "Pour out Your fury on the Gentiles, who do not know You, and on the families who do not call on Your name," (Jer. 10:25). When your family does not call out to God, your family mimics the Atheist and pagan who regularly do not do so. God's fury rests on such families. What do you think of a person who generally offends God, that does not worship God, (Zechariah 14:17), that does not call on the name of the Lord, (Psalm 14:4; Isaiah 64:7), that does not come to the Church, (2 Chronicles 29:6-7), that does

---

[14] "You are likely to see no general Reformation, until you procure family Reformation. Some little obscure Religion there may be in here and there one; but while it sticks in single persons, and is not promoted by these societies, it doth not prosper, nor promise much for future increase." Baxter, Richard, *The Reformed Pastor*, (London: Robert White, for Nevil Simmons, 1656) 86-87.

not have devotions, that does not pray with his family, (Jeremiah 10:25). Such a one is called an *atheist*. When your family acts like that family, it is acting contrary to the righteousness of God. Which means that you must keep out (as much as you are able) all wicked people from your houses. It is relatively impossible to keep up the Christian faith in your families, in power and holiness when swearers, drunks, agnostics, atheists and those who scoff at godliness dwell inside. Such kinds of people will corrupt your children and family members. Such kinds of people will mock you and quench your devotional time. Prayers and catechizing must sometimes be left off to gratify them. Sabbaths are profaned for their sakes. Daniel Cawdrey said about federal heads, "Say then, you masters of houses, "Away from me, all who are wicked, I will keep the commandments of my God." Even strangers of old were to be kept from profaning the Sabbath, as in the fourth commandment; the stranger that is within your gates. Or if not, to be sent out your doors, out of your gates, (Nehemiah 13:17, 21). If they will not observe the religious service of the house, do not let them stay in your houses. Say peremptorily, say and hold it. "As for you, do what you think is good, be wicked and profane, as you will, but as for me and my house, we will serve the Lord."[15]

---

[15] See Daniel Cawdrey's whole work, *Family Reformation Promoted*, published by Puritan Publications.

Some objections come up when we consider family worship. Someone may say, "We pray, that's enough!" No, that is not enough, where one duty will not supply all the needs and benefits of all other duties – it does not spiritually work that way. Heads of households are commanded to teach your household the righteousness of God.

"I get embarrassed to lead my family, I'm not that smart." That's really only a matter of preparation of some kind. Study, memorize Scriptures, and the like. Use sermons, books, study tools, the advice of ministers of what to study, what might be helpful to you. Seek it out and be prepared. It is not a scholar's lesson, it is suited to the family. Don't overcomplicate it in the beginning.

"We are too busy at home, not everyone is always there, and we just don't have time." Does family prayer get in the way of your job? Is that the excuse one might use with your boss? Why would one use it with God? Does family worship get in the way of mowing the lawn? Or in the way of movie night? Teaching your family about God *is the business of your life.* It would be better to lack sleep, food and other things before it would be better to lack what God has specifically commanded of his people in this regard. The family altar is never to be neglected. If God sees you are not serious about this, who knows what he may do in hindering your worldly business or lives with all sorts of things. Financial trouble, sickness, injury, job loss, *etc.* We already read it once, but here it is again, "Pour out Your fury on the

Gentiles, who do not know You, and on the families who do not call on Your name," (Jer. 10:25). Define in your own mind the idea of God's fury. Don't let your heritage be like Eli's, "Now the sons of Eli were corrupt; they did not know the LORD," (1 Sam. 2:12).

When you as a Christian give excuses not to have daily family worship, you make God out to wink at sin, as if he will "give an okay" to your impiety. To neglect family worship is to charge God with injustice. "Now consider this, you who forget God, Lest I tear you in pieces, and there be none to deliver," (Psa. 50:22).

Family-worship is a duty mandated by God on you who are covenant heads, every day, and especially upon the Lord's Day. There are various Scriptural aspects that show you as a family that worship is to be done by the family in this way, much less this pattern and precept by Abraham. The Passover was celebrated by families, (Exodus 12:3). Prophecies in the Old Testament point to family worship. "At the same time," says the LORD, "I will be the God of all the families of Israel, and they shall be My people," (Jer. 31:1). All those who served God in the Bible worshipped together with their family. Adam, Noah, Abraham, Joshua, *etc.*, all did this. Oliver Heywood, says, "Another argument for a family-altar is, that the providence of God calls for it; "God setteth the solitary in families," Psalm 98:6."[16] The church today often wants to rip the family apart and

---

[16] Heywood, *Works*, Volume 4, 433.

individualize salvation, covenant, and service. In contrast, Jesus Christ is a God of families who serve him.

Family worship distinguishes those who serve Christ and God, and those who are worldly. "...there may not be among you man or woman or family or tribe, whose heart turns away today from the LORD our God, to go and serve the gods of these nations, and that there may not be among you a root bearing bitterness or wormwood," (Deut. 29:18). How, then, does your family *act* like a little church? How do you who are federal heads of your family enact such blessings? It is especially to be done on the Lord's Day. The week should be highlighted on that day. Take time to go over sermons, teachings and such. Even catching up on things from the week in your devotions that you might have skipped, and help others do the same.

Family worship is a hearty means to find Christ. Christ is the God of families, (have you thought about this?) families should worship him. He founded families and instructs families and does so at even a greater extent in the fulfillment of Jesus Christ in the New Covenant. Not less, *but more so.* If there is more light, there is more responsibility, more instruction in righteousness as Abraham did. God's covenantal design is depositing the elect in families. Christ came to seek and save that which is lost. He does so by seeking out the lost sheep, those part of the fold of God's covenant. Where does he go to find them?

Families are integral in relation to God's covenant blessings. God generally does not design the promise of salvation to lone rangers. He certainly saves people out of families, where, in many instances, the whole family is not necessarily converted, but one child might be, and then it is their duty to propagate that. Yet, Scripturally, covenant families are constantly seen in God's designs where they consistently exist to serve God. Adam's family, Noah's family, Abraham's family, Isaac's family, Jacob's family, Moses' family, Joshua's family, *etc.* God sees your family as exceedingly important. A little church, with a little governance to propagate *godly seed*, as he says in Malachi 2:15. And as mentioned by Christ, "Jesus said, "Let the little children come to Me, and do not forbid them; for of such is the kingdom of heaven." And he laid his hands on them and departed from there," (Matt. 19:14-15). The kingdom belongs to babies. They in turn are blessed by God, they are not treated as heathen as many churches want to do, they are treated as blessed disciples. Your covenant family matters to God in that way because God works by way of covenant with them. How important is this to you? How much time do you take to teach them the way of righteousness and justice, like father Abraham? How do you teach them about Christ's righteousness, the epitome of God's work to distribute his salvation to individuals in your family through his everlasting covenant that he had with Abraham?

There are a great many blessings to be found in Christ in worshipping and studying and praying with your family. Your family is hidden under the shadow of the almighty – there you find protection in Christ. Your family is set within the providence of God's provision – there you are provided for by Christ, the commander of the wheels.[17] Your family is placed within the context of the way of peace – there your family relations improve through Christ, the door, the wicket gate one passes through onto the road of salvation. Your family is established within the context of the covenant of grace – there your children will come to know Christ more intimately. Your family, then, can be both a catalyst in the church and in the community, to further making Christ their chief end, and reforming your part of the world.[18]

---

[17] Ezekiel 10:13.

[18] "A great neglect there hath been of family reformation in our city; how few have with Joshua resolved, and accordingly endeavored that they and their houses should serve the Lord? How few have set up religious worship in their families? Have not many hundred houses in the city been without family-prayer in them from one end of the week to the other? And is it strange that the Lord hath burned down those houses, wherein the inhabitants would not vouchsafe to worship him? And where there hath been some prayer in many families, it was but once a day, and that so late at night, and when the body hath been so tried, and sleepy, and the soul so dull, and unfit for Gods service, that the prayers have been no prayers, or lost prayers, such, which instead of pleasing him, have provoked him to anger? How few did labor to instruct their families; catechize their children and servants, to bring them up in the nurture and admonition of the Lord? Hath not God threatened to pour out his wrath upon irreligious families? Jeremiah 10:25." Vincent, Thomas, *God's Terrible Voice in the City*, (London: s.n., 1667) 136-137.

Your family altar is a commanded necessity. What do you sacrifice to God on it? It should be the shining star of your home. God will say of you, *I know him. I know him, and his devotion to me, and I know the devotion of his family. He commands his children and his household after his own piety and religion, and he keeps my way, the way of the LORD, to teach his family about me, my righteousness, my justice, all my judgments, and in return, I have brought the blessing of the Covenant Testator on him, my one and only Son Jesus, that I bring upon him all that I have promised in my covenant to those who are faithful.*

Mark 5: Family Worship Part 2

Catechizing in the Church

"Train up a child in the way he should go: and when he is old, he will not depart from it," (Prov. 22:6).

Proverbs is a compilation of wise sayings, this one in chapter 22 being said of Solomon. Proverbs is part of what is classified as wisdom literature. In this particular section of Scripture, we have the "wise sayings" of Solomon. "And God gave Solomon wisdom and exceedingly great understanding, and largeness of heart like the sand on the seashore," (1 Kings 4:29). The wise sayings of Solomon cover almost every principled aspect of life. He deals with, in this very chapter of Proverbs alone, humility, reputation, creation, debt, sloth, discipline, wisdom, knowledge, emotional stability, heritage and a number of other proverbial wise sayings. This section of Proverbs actually begins quite a few chapters back in 10:1 which cover the first section of Solomon's wise sayings, and within these sayings show forth the difference between a wise son and foolish son. It causes the reader to consider, since it is merely a series of proverbs, what kind of son or daughter, are you?

The text says, "Train up a child in the way he should go, and when he is old he will not depart from it," (Prov. 22:6). Set a child right at the entrance of his way, literally. It has the idea of a path, and from early beginnings that path ought to be set down. This means the instructor must know the way for the student. It assumes there is someone who knows the path, who has gone down the path, and who can teach the path; who initially has received this path and can refer to this path as God instructs. It means that the way is set according to God's word, and such a path is to be followed. If one were to give a syllable by syllable rendering of the Hebrew word "train up" it means to "put something into the child's mouth." Something in this way must be chewed, tasted, swallowed and digested otherwise such food would never profit. It is a kind of nourishment and nursing for them. So, it has the idea of elementary instruction that the child can understand and grow by it. They are to learn and understand progressively, so any of those instructed receive instruction based on their level of understanding. One would never teach a 5-year-old the same things in the same way that they would teach a 16-year-old. Discernment in teaching well is important in this. It is eminently experiential, as taste always is. They must experience it, they must taste it as it's put into their mouth. If that path is set and trod, it will become ingrained in the child and when further age overtakes him, in all the ages of his life, the familiar path is the one in which the child should remain.

This is a *Proverb* – all things being equal, if they are trained in this way, set on the right path, they should, for all intents and purposes continue on that path when they are older. Such experience in this kind of teaching should be habit forming. For someone to teach someone else a habit takes a great amount of care and responsibility. It also takes into account the idea of ignorance in a certain respect. The child is taught a certain way and doesn't know, at the time, any other way than what they are taught. It builds and guides on ignorance to bring them to the point of understanding and experimental knowledge. It removes ignorance and replaces it with God's judgments. This is the same idea Christ uses when he tells the Pharisees that "Woe to you, scribes and Pharisees, hypocrites! For you travel land and sea to win one convert, and when he is won, you make him twice as much a son of hell as yourselves," (Matt. 23:15)." They create converts that are twice as bad as they are because those converts only know what they are being taught by the hypocrites. When such teaching occurs under false teachers and such, this can be a terrible thing. This is the case with cults. This is the case with *many* "evangelical" churches today. But when such teaching occurs that is in direct alignment with the word of God, spiritual benefits occur.

"Foolishness is bound up in the heart of a child; The rod of correction will drive it far from him," (Prov. 22:15). This verse 15 is a commentary - considered with verse 6, it shows that children will indeed have folly or foolishness bound up in them and certain aspects of corporeal discipline are required to drive it from them. Yet, still, this is early on. The way the child should be instructed is not something that can wait until they are older. They must be fully prepared, early. And such instruction cannot simply be "I told you so" but it must surround the teaching that accompanies Scripture and authority; without which, there is no authority. In conjunction with verse 6, if one gets the folly out of a child in the beginning, the child will continue on the right way. Folly must be purged so that paths may be straight, and not crooked. The work of the Messiah makes crooked paths straight in this light, even for children. There is an argument contained in the directive where the first part of the proverb is explained with the argument of the last part. Train up...and when he is old. Training is the argument. The conclusion to training is that they will in fact walk the path when they are old. Yet, consider, it is a *proverb*. Again, all things being equal, train up a child, and when he is old he will remain in that way.

The words "train up" may also be rightly understood as *catechize*. Catechize means "instruction by word of mouth." One who is catechized is instructed by teaching. The original meaning of the word is to make *someone learn by teaching orally*, which is the origin of the Latin term. As a verb in English, it's found to mean: teach or examine by means of questions and answers. These questions and answers help students learn what they are being taught. Catechize a child in the way he should go, and when he is old he shall not depart from it, is a fine rendering of the idea. Moving from catechizing to the doctrine extracted from the text is a bit broader.

DOCTRINE: Superiors have the fundamental duty to wisely train up or catechize all inferiors who are providentially obligated to their care by God. These carefully chosen words echo the *Westminster Larger* and *Shorter Catechisms.* Using terms like "superior and inferior" are not any kind of ill-willed terminology. It is not putting anyone down. These terms simply designate those educated and those not educated who need to be educated. However, superior and inferior allow for a broad stroke in a number of different areas when speaking about teaching, ruling, obedience, submission and the like. They can allude to people in the church. Pastors and elders are teachers or rulers *over* the congregation. In the family there are...parents and children. At work there are masters and slaves as Paul explains in Ephesians 5 or, simply bosses and employees. There are also inferiors and superiors among peers. Paul to Timothy is a superior to Timothy as a pastoral guide. Students are subject to teachers in a university, and so on. In this case of the *proverb*, it is specifically those who teach and those who learn. Teachers and students. Here is found training children to grow up to be godly adults. And for the purposes of the proverb, it is specifically superior teachers over inferior children who are taught a way of life before others and before God. It is the heart of the book of wisdom literature in Proverbs to accomplish this: rendering the heart pliable to God's word and will. Question 118 in the *Westminster Larger Catechism* asks, "Why is the charge of keeping the sabbath more specially directed to governors of families, and other *superiors?*"

Question 125, "Why are superiors styled Father and Mother?" Answer, "Superiors are styled Father and Mother, both to teach them in all duties toward their inferiors..." Question 64, "What is required in the fifth commandment?" Answer, "The fifth commandment requireth the preserving the honor, and performing the duties, belonging to everyone in their several places and relations, as superiors, inferiors, or equals." These terms simply help understand God given roles.

Those who are superior are over those inferior. Superiors are concerned for the inferior's spiritual and temporal good. They do this first in nourishing them well, providing all needful things for life and health. "Now Israel loved Joseph more than all his children, because he was the son of his old age. Also he made him a tunic of many colors," (Gen. 37:3). "The streets of the city shall be full of boys and girls playing in its streets," (Zech. 8:5). "Or what man is there among you who, if his son asks for bread, will give him a stone?" Such superiors nurture inferiors with good manners. "You shall rise before the gray headed and honor the presence of an old man, and fear your God: I am the LORD," (Lev. 19:32). "Do not exalt yourself in the presence of the king, And do not stand in the place of the great," (Prov. 25:6). "When you are invited by anyone to a wedding feast, do not sit down in the best place, lest one more honorable than you be invited by him," (Luke 14:8). They are even taught to learn how to succeed in some honest calling. "Then his brothers went to feed their father's flock in Shechem," (Gen. 37:12). "Now the priest of Midian had seven daughters. And they came and drew water, and they filled the troughs to water their father's flock," (Exod. 2:16). Superiors, in this Proverb, are concerned for the inferior's spiritual good. *In admonition of the Lord.* "For I have known him, in order that he may command his children and his household after him, that they keep the way of the LORD, to do righteousness and justice, that the LORD may bring to Abraham what he has spoken to him," (Gen. 18:19). "Only take heed to yourself, and diligently keep yourself, lest you forget the things your eyes have seen, and lest they depart from your heart all the days of your life. And teach them to your children and your grandchildren," (Deut. 4:9). "He also taught me, and said to me: "Let your heart retain my words; Keep my commands, and live. Get wisdom! Get understanding! Do not forget, nor turn away from the words of my mouth," (Prov. 4:4-5). "... when I call to remembrance the genuine faith that is in you, which dwelt first in your grandmother Lois and your mother Eunice, and I am persuaded is in you also," (2 Tim. 1:5).

In reading the word, "and that from childhood you have known the Holy Scriptures, which are able to make you wise for salvation through faith which is in Christ Jesus," (2 Timothy 3:15). In catechizing, "You shall teach them diligently to your children, and shall talk of them when you sit in your house, when you walk by the way, when you lie down, and when you rise up," (Deut. 6:7).

By an exemplary life, "Then they came to the children of Reuben, to the children of Gad, and to half the tribe of Manasseh, to the land of Gilead, and they spoke with them, saying, "Thus says the whole congregation of the LORD: `What treachery is this that you have committed against the God of Israel, to turn away this day from following the LORD, in that you have built for yourselves an altar, that you might rebel this day against the LORD?" (Josh. 22:15-16).

At what age does all this best occur? It should start with *the child*. What is a child? It can mean an infant newly born, (Judges 13:7;) of three months old, (Exod. 2:6;) a child as soon as he begins to speak and exert his reason. In this way it runs parallel with the New Testament Greek word βρεφος; and so we find Timothy instructed απο βρεφους, "from a child," a little one, (2 Tim. 1:5, with 3:15.). He learned from the time of being a little one what it meant to be a godly Christian. And consider that such learning from the Scriptures was from the Old Testament. There is found, then, various stages, and levels of wisdom which are used to instruct little ones based on age.

Who are superiors? Those of the family, or those of the church. In the *Larger and Shorter Catechism* descriptions of superiors runs both to parents, and to church leaders. Consider the nature of the Pastoral Ministry as Feeders (Shepherds) who Feed the flock.

Jeremiah 3:15, "Shepherds who will feed you with knowledge and understanding." This is catechizing. One of the most famous systematic theology books ever written, one of the top four, along with Calvin's *Institutes*, William Ames' *Marrow of Theology*, and the Westminster Standards, was by a theologian named Francis Turretin. *Institutes of Elenctic Theology* is its name, and its massive three volumes were written in *catechistic form* to teach families theology, by questions and answers.

The church in the Old Testament constantly taught by way of catechizing. "And teach them to your children and your grandchildren," (Deut. 4:9). "... that they may teach their children," (Deut. 4:10). "You shall teach them diligently to your children," (Deut. 6:7). "You shall teach them to your children, speaking of them when you sit in your house, when you walk by the way, when you lie down, and when you rise up," (Deut. 11:19). "... and teach it to the children of Israel; put it in their mouths," (Deut. 31:19). Jesus catechized constantly in his sermons and instruction. "...what reward have you?" (Matt. 5:46). "...what do you do more than others?" (Matt. 5:47). "What did you go out into the wilderness to see? A reed shaken by the wind?" (Matt. 11:7). "But to what shall I liken this generation?" (Matt. 11:16). "For what will it profit a man if he gains the whole world, and loses his own soul?" (Mark 8:36). "What did Moses command you?" (Mark 10:3). "What is written in the law?" (Luke 10:26). "What then is this that is written:

The stone which the builders rejected Has become the chief cornerstone?" (Luke 20:17). The Apostles all catechized in this same way. Paul catechized. He says, "But we were gentle among you, just as a nursing mother cherishes her own children," (1 Thess. 2:7). Paul compares himself to *a nursing mother*. A nursing mother cares for and nurtures the children. He considered himself a builder of the people. "According to the grace of God which was given to me, as a wise master builder I have laid the foundation, and another builds on it," (1 Cor. 3:10). Peter catechized. He was personally instructed by Christ to teach and feed Christ's blood bought church. "Jesus said to Simon Peter, "Simon, son of Jonah, do you love Me more than these?" He said to him, "Yes, Lord; You know that I love You." He said to him, "Feed My lambs."" (John 21:15). "Therefore, laying aside all malice, all deceit, hypocrisy, envy, and all evil speaking, as newborn babes, desire the pure milk of the word, that you may grow thereby, if indeed you have tasted that the Lord is gracious," (1 Peter 2:1-3). His thought was feeding or nursing the people in this way. *To teach them*. The writer of Hebrews catechized. "For though by this time you ought to be teachers, you need someone to teach you again the first principles of the oracles of God; and you have come to need milk and not solid food," (Heb. 5:12). He assumes that they should be superiors when in fact they are still inferiors. Such a sad commentary on their spiritual growth. Consider the family, "And these words which I command you today shall be in your heart. You shall teach them diligently to your children, and shall talk of them when you sit in your house, when you walk by the way, when you lie down, and when you rise up," (Deut. 6:6-7). And of course Proverbs 22:6! In the family, catechizing is to take place, training up. When? When you lie down, rise up, all the time, every day. Consider that training up a child concerns the future of the church. What will the church be like in 50 years? Part time Christians by part time teaching? *Part?* What paths are being taught? What paths are being neglected? What preparations are being made? What commands are being replaced or abandoned?

The end of catechizing is a theology of walking. Paths are for *walking.* The idea of the proverb is very clear – set one walking on the path of righteousness that leads to Christ, all the time. The end of catechizing is a closer walk with Christ to demonstrate glory to his name on earth, all the time. This is to not depart from the true path which is through him and leads to him. *Not* departing from God's Path. Not departing from Jesus Christ. Rather, like an olive in the press, *pressed into Christ.* God desires godly seed that are trained up, taught, catechized according to his word.[1] "He seeks

---

[1] "Consider. Whether God hath not committed unto you a guardianship over the souls of your families, and it be not upon that account your duty to take care for the discharge of theirs?" *The Address of some ministers of Christ in the Isle of Wight & County of Southampton to the people of their respective charges, by way of exhortation, to discharge their parts of those two great and*

godly offspring. Therefore take heed to your spirit, And let none deal treacherously with the wife of his youth," (Mal. 2:15). Not *part time godly offspring*. Order the family in such a way as to fulfill being fruitful and multiply on the earth in a godly and holy manner, to raise up a family that infects the world with godly seed.

How are inferiors to be trained up by superiors? Train up a child "in the mouth of his way." Feeding in a certain capacity needful spiritual food. That means according to what the child can handle. It must have in mind the spirit and ability of the child so that the child can learn rightly. One would not, for example, take a five-year-old and ask them to begin reciting the *Larger Catechism* immediately. In some ways, the same goes for adults. Again, "For though by this time you ought to be teachers, you need someone to teach you again the first principles of the oracles of God; and you have come to need milk and not solid food," (Heb. 5:12). The very fact that the writer says this is given in the next verse. "For everyone who partakes only of milk is unskilled in the word of righteousness, for he is a babe," (Heb. 5:13). Skill must be cultivated. Cultivation occurs in the context of the three spiritual disciplines privately, during daily family worship, and during public worship corporately. That is why there is a *Shorter* catechism and a *Larger* catechism because it takes into account the spirit, disposition and ability of the seven year old mind, or

---

necessary duties, private conference and catechizing, (London: J.H. for J. Rothwell, 1658) 8.

those who need to learn first principles, as well as higher thoughts of God.

The training of theology should be considered as well. Consider that the *Larger and Shorter Catechisms* begin, not with spiritual disciplines of personal devotion, but with theological instruction. They begin with knowing the Bible, who God is, who Christ is, what Christ has done, *etc.*, far before they ever get to spiritual disciplines of reading, praying and meditating, or even worship. To not understand the former will never give way to the latter done well. Not just "... a form of sound words;" (2 Tim. 1:13;) but, "a form of sound words," which contained "the principles of the doctrine of Christ," and "the first principles of the oracles of God."

There must be training in the basic spiritual disciplines. Consider, that the *Larger and Shorter Catechisms* also teach spiritual disciplines. What is the practical nature of the Moral Law? How should one pray? How should one read the word? How should one study? How should one meditate on the word?

Training in this capacity, then, is a mode of spiritual *discipleship*. John Brown said, "one, must be a disciple indeed, in order to be fruitful, or to continue in Christ's word. It is not fruitfulness that creates true discipleship. It is true discipleship that produces fruitfulness. Continuance in Christ's word is necessary to constitute true discipleship, there could be no true disciples, for it is plain a man must, as a true disciple, first receive Christ's word in order to continue in it."[2] Jesus instructs the disciples (his chosen apostles) to make other *disciples* in Matthew 28; make *disciples* not *converts*. How Christ had longed and desired to gather the children of Jerusalem! He yearns that they be *gathered of one mind in this way.* He longed to make disciples of them all, to instruct them all, and have them, in turn instruct others. Churches often mistake discipleship for some sort of rudimentary "Sunday School" class. Making disciples has particular steps and relations. It has many levels, and it goes on until one no longer needs to be taught. How long is that? To say one does not need to be a disciple is to say one does not need to be a Christian. Such are joined together in practical application.

Training up children in the home is primarily accomplished by parents. The verse in Proverbs specifically is set in the overall context of children and parents. 23 times Solomon uses the term "my son." Children are important to parents, and to God, as a godly heritage. They are not to be ushered off to Sunday School in neglect of the family teaching the children. Children are part of the believer's household. God said to Abraham, "And I will establish my covenant between me and thee and thy seed after thee in their generations for an everlasting covenant, to be a God unto thee, and to thy seed after thee," (Gen. 17:7). Two basic premises

---

[2] Brown, John, *Discourses and Sayings of Our Lord Jesus Christ*, Volume 2, (New York: Robert Carter and Brothers, 1854) 404.

can be taken out of this verse, and many others like it. God considers children, or the seed of believers, important enough to specifically say he will be a God to them even before their birth. Parents of the children of believers are to take special note of God's intention to their children as those in God's covenant. God's covenant is set in the context of catechizing. This does not mean that children bypass being totally depraved, or affected with Adam's sin. As a matter of fact, such a verse and such concepts affirm the truth of total depravity, not deny it. Children are born under the curse, and they are fallen and completely affected in their mind, body and soul with the sin of Adam, and this aggravates the eternal consequences of sin in their personal disobedience. They must be trained up. Training presupposes being fallen and sinful. Jonathan Edwards called them, as the saying goes, vipers in diapers.[3] Parents of covenant children, however, depend on God's promise that their children are considered differently in the Covenant of Grace. They are holy and set apart (1 Corinthians 7:14). They are to be taught and trained.[4] Otherwise, they would never be able to teach them the

---

[3] Edwards, *Works*, (Yale), Volume 3, 422-423.

[4] If they are not to be taught and trained the ways of God, one must reconcile the idea that children are to be considered heathen with the command that God has given them to teach them. But the heathen, "Because the carnal mind is enmity against God: for it is not subject to the law of God, neither indeed can be," (Rom. 8:7). Does God treat them as heathen who are at enmity with him? If so, why would be command households to be taught and trained up in the ways of God?

Bible. Really? Yes. The Bible is the way they should walk before God and be blameless as a covenant household. But if they do not consider their children as Christians, or in the covenant with God, why would they teach them the Bible as Christians would be taught? How could they? "Because the carnal mind is enmity against God; for it is not subject to the law of God, nor indeed can be. So then, those who are in the flesh cannot please God." (Rom. 8:7-8). To assume otherwise is to disregard training them up. God would be requiring them to train something untrainable because they are at enmity with God. How does one train up a depraved mind? It's impossible. It is at enmity; it is a God hater. Those kinds of mind need the preaching of Gospel to be transformed by the renewing of the Spirit. But *God requires* the training of godly seed; which is a complete and utter overthrow of the neglect of children as part of the visible church. With such a daunting responsibility as to be good stewards of holy covenant children, it is the parent's responsibility (not the local Sunday school class) to teach them how to be good Christians before the face of God. Parenting does not only include physical correction and training to obey parents (such as eating all their dinner that is placed in front of them), but more specifically spiritual correction and godly discipline. God says, "Gather me the people together, and I will make them hear my words, that they may learn to fear me all the days that they shall live upon the earth, and that they may teach their children," (Deut. 4:10).

167

Jesus was especially concerned with covenant children and their well-being when he said, in one place, "Suffer the little children to come unto me, and forbid them not: for of such belongs the kingdom of God," (Mark 10:14). This verse, and Matthew 19:14 which quotes Mark 10:14, uses the term "such a one" to refer to children. Children carry great weight in God's covenant.

Thomas Lye, a puritan, quotes Eusebius, that there was one set apart on purpose for this office in the primitive church, called "the catechist," *qui catechismum docebat,* and others called *catechumen,* "that learned the catechism;" and these were of two sorts. (1.) Jews and Heathens, that offered themselves to be listed among the Christians, and were not as yet sufficiently seen in the great fundamentals of the Christian religion. (2.) The children of believing parents that had been baptized. Lye says, "Both these were put under the careful institution of the catechist, and by him to be so far instructed, till they had attained so much knowledge in the principles of the Christian religion, as that the Heathens might be admitted to baptism, and the Christian children to the Lord's Supper."[5] Such a requirement to the superior to train the inferior is a basic Christian exercise as God has set it up in the church, and in the little church, the family.

---

[5] Lye, Thomas, "By what Scriptural rules may catechizing be so managed..." Edited by Nichols, James, *Puritan Sermons,* Volume 2, (Wheaton, IL: Richard Owen Roberts, Publishers, 1981) 104.

God gives a command to train up or disciple your children in the way or manner of their life. If God and Christ hold such a high regard for children and godly seed, so should we. They are the future of the church, and they are those who "belong" to the kingdom of heaven. They are designed, as we are, to glorify God and his only Son Jesus Christ. Being a child is not a negative or bad thing. Jesus Christ, as an infant, *was head of the visible and invisible church.* Christ, in his incarnation, as a child, was the sovereign Lord of the church. Being an infant did not make him *not* so. The age of human flesh is not relevant in terms of covenant. What was all that great honor given to Christ as an infant in his birth? Scriptural prophecies were fulfilled when he was conceived and born. Prophecies given and gifts from Magi. Heralding by Angels. Witnesses like the shepherds in the city. The savior, as a baby, was God and Lord. What is age to that but a linear restriction placed on a faulty idea that children are somehow not part of the visible church? As much as Christ was not head of it as an infant! And if Christ may be head of the church as a baby, children *belong* (Jesus' words) to the church and may be members of the visible church. For such belongs the kingdom of heaven. Do you see your children in this way? Are they so important?

Scripture tells us that if we train up our children in the way they should go, when they are old they will not depart from those teachings. All things being equal, this is not an easy task, but it is a commanded one. Do you believe that? "Train up a child..." (Proverbs 22:6). Some say, *It's too hard, I don't want to.* Then why did you have children? There is in Scripture a theology of children, and God seeks from parents: "godly offspring," (Mal. 2:15). God seeks you to deal faithfully with the wife of your youth to procure for the kingdom in dominion, godly offspring. "Behold, children are a heritage from the LORD, the fruit of the womb is a reward," (Psa. 127:3). God gives you children to be a heritage to him and for you. And he desires that such a heritage is not trained up in evil, but in the way of righteousness. "They have dealt treacherously with the LORD, For they have begotten pagan children. Now a New Moon shall devour them and their heritage," (Hos. 5:7). This was God's judgment against Israel and Judah for mishandling the church and leading their children down the wrong path.

Consider their state. They are young and in need of training. Responsibility, then, lies on you to train them. They come forth from the womb speaking lies, as the Psalmist says, but not speaking the truth. They must be taught the truth because Adam's sin and curse lies upon them, which dissuades them from even considering it. They do not need to learn evil. They are born with that. You don't have to teach them to be bad. They simply learn how to be worse. They need your instruction.

You are to train your children wisely beginning sooner than later. The fear of the Lord is the beginning of wisdom (Prov. 9:10). It is not enough that you train yourself, but that to be a good father or mother to your children, you train them. Such training is twofold. You are to train your children physically, and you train your children spiritually. It rests on you to fulfill this with all gravity.

Training is connected with blessings. There is a connection between success in this and the promised blessing. Think about Abraham, "For I have known him, in order that he may command his children and his household after him, that they keep the way of the LORD, to do righteousness and justice, that the LORD may bring to Abraham what He has spoken to him," (Gen. 18:19). Train up and govern your family religiously in the way of the Lord.[6] Walk with your family as joint-heirs of the covenant of grace. Raise your children in the nurture and admonition of the Lord, having them in subjection with all gravity. Teach them to serve the Lord Jesus Christ, and give to them what is just before God. Your family is to be a *little church*. Family-worship in all its parts should be diligently preserved in this way. It is the training up of those in the Way of Christ. From the time you lie down to the time you wake up. There are armchair theologians all over the internet and reformed

---

[6] "Take heed of filling their heads with whimzies, and unprofitable notions; for this will sooner learn them to be malepert and proud, than sober and humble. Open therefore to them the state of man by nature: discourse with them of sin, of death, and hell; of a crucified Savior, and the promise of life through faith." Bunyan, John, *Christian Behavior, or, The fruits of True Christianity,* (London: Printed for F. Smith, ND) 56.

chat boards telling people that this is not something Christian families need to do each day. But mark this, the days they don't do it, they don't do it when they get up or lie down, they act as *atheists*. Atheists don't ever do it. Francis Roberts, "This was Abraham's practice and praise. But if you do not have due care of the souls committed to your charge, if you have no family worship among your household, no reading of Scriptures, no catechizing, no praying, no religious conversation; no visible memorials of God, Jesus Christ, or Christianity, how do you differ from the families of mere pagans and infidels? You are quite degenerate from Abraham. What do you do more for your household, then the very brute beasts for their young, providing only for back and belly, and this present life? Abraham did not do this."[7] To depart from this training, from this family altar, is to engage in practical atheism.[8]

Job was concerned for his family, even in sacrificing for them on their behalf. Spiritual disciplines were first and foremost on his mind on behalf of his children, "Thus Job did regularly," (Job 1:5).

Joshua, "But as for me and my house, we will serve the LORD," (Josh. 24:15). Service in the ways of God is service to God. Wholly giving up everything in

---

[7] Roberts, Francis, *Mysterium & Medulla Bibliorum*, (London: R.W. for George Calvert, 1657) 433.

[8] "If you neglect to instruct them in the way of the Lord, Satan, and their own natural corruptions, will not fail to instruct them in the way to hell." Flavel, John, *Husbandry Spiritualized*, (London: Printed by Robert Boulter, 1674) 202.

relation to what God desires for a godly family and instruction.

The sad case of Eli. To not do this training, is to have one of the saddest commentaries that could be given, laid on you and your family. "Now the sons of Eli were corrupt; they did not know the LORD," (1 Sam. 2:12). Eli was a priest. What did he teach his children? Form and function? Where was the heart of the word to lead them to cling and hold steadfastly to the ways of the coming Messiah? They were corrupt. They did not know the Lord.

Finally, all superiors to inferiors are to be taught for the good of the church. The broad stroke of this verse is the business of religion to become infectious; training others. A providential care of inferiors for their temporal good, is in turn for their eternal good. Christ was always about teaching the people of God for their good. He taught all his disciples, and those that would learn from them, through various methods of Scriptural instruction to bring them to a higher understanding of declaring the Father and his will. All of this training and teaching is to bring you into a worshipful demeanor and make you godly seed, that in time sharpens others. Jesus taught his disciples to consider their lives and his teachings inside the context of the coming of his Kingdom which was not only now, but not yet. Such training should be done according to sound instruction and the Bible. Such a training should be done plainly so that others can understand it. Such training should be done daily, constantly, when you lie down to when you rise, when you go in and when you go out.

Inferiors should take special care in making such training advantageous for them. As inferiors, you must think first, you cannot be trained up before God without first being in Christ. Your evil heart must be tamed by Christ first. Christ's life and death are God's accepted covering for you. The way of the Messiah covers you and God then sees you under his covering. That is the straight and narrow way, not the crooked path. All your works before God are crooked. All your duties before him are bent. God requires them all to be perfectly straight. That is the path, that is the only way. But this is not something you can do on your own. You must gain an interest, above all other things in Christ and his will for your life. This is the way you as children must be trained up. Disciples are blessed with the whole blessing of Christ, in Christ. All of it, lacking nothing, in him. He gives you all his blessings by his holy Spirit. It is not just the blessings themselves which you may be blessed with, but the entirety of the spiritual blessing in Christ.

Those in Christ receive grace; those outside do not. Those outside of Christ have no spiritual blessings unless they have the one complete spiritual blessing in Christ which is given upon salvation. He does not require much of you. He does not require you to climb a mountain. He does not require you to defeat a whole army. He does not require you to pay a great amount of money. He says, "Look to Me, and be saved," (Isa. 45:22).

The blessing of Christ's blood cries to you to *look* to him. Each drop of his blood cries out to you to believe in him, look to him, and follow him. Have an interest in him above all things, and believe that he will save you. Keep in mind that the Spirit of God has placed this directive in Scripture for your good, and the good of your family. God desires you train up godly seed. This is his will. Your will and God's will need to match up. You may not know all the things God wants you to know, but he has given you superiors that will help you learn the truth and walk in it, so that in the coming years you will hold onto that teaching as something you find most important.

Lastly, in this, honor your elders, your parents, your superiors that they would not find it burdensome to teach you and instruct you in the right way. Don't make learning difficult. It is that which sets before you the narrow way that is straight, because as you know, all those crooked ways lead you to mouth of hell. Though the way of salvation may be difficult and hard at times, it is still the best way, the only way, in which you should be trained up, and never to depart from it.

FINIS

Other Books in the 5 Marks Series at Puritan Publications

5 Marks of Biblical Reformation
Everybody loves to claim the magisterial reformation for their own! Everyone wants to be a reformer in that way. But take God's principles of a Biblical Reformation and apply them to the church in practical daily living, then that's a different story all together.

5 Marks of Biblical Commitment to the Visible Body of Christ
Are you a member of Christ's church? Are you a covenanter? Do you support your church? Are you committed to it? How do you show it?

5 Marks of a Biblical Disciple
What is a disciple? A disciple has "5 Marks" outlined in Scripture which demonstrate a Spirit-filled walking with Jesus Christ in newness of life.

5 Marks of a Biblical Church
What are the marks of a biblical church? There are 5 marks that demonstrate the church as the pillar and ground of the truth.